BACK TO THE GARDEN

BACK TO THE GARDEN

BRIAN P. LUCAS

© 2025 by Family Priority Publishing

All rights reserved. No part of this publication may be reproduced, distributed, or transmitted in any form or by any means, including photocopying, recording, or other electronic or mechanical methods, without the prior written permission of the publisher, except in the case of brief quotations embodied in critical reviews and certain other noncommercial uses permitted by copyright law.

All Scripture quotations are from the King James Version of the Bible.

Brian P. Lucas is not a licensed and/or registered rabbi, preacher, bishop, priest, deacon, minister, teacher, theologian, seminary student or attendant, psychologist, therapist, or counselor and is in no way, shape, or form promoting a man-made religion, denomination, or church and/or providing you with any earthly religious advice in any capacity. All subject matter provided herein is for spiritual informational purposes only. Brian P. Lucas does not guarantee you results. You and only you are responsible for what you do or don't do with the spiritual and biblical information provided, so due diligence on your part is an expected and appreciated requirement.

Family Priority Publishing
66 W Flagler St
Suite 900 PMB #10522
Miami, Florida 33130

ISBN:
978-1-7324104-2-8
10 9 8 7 6 5 4 3 2 1

Printed in the United States of America

Lifetime Thanks

To Jan G. Lucas, who believes in me, cares for me, and loves me unconditionally, even when I do not know or understand how to believe in, care for, or love myself — a strong woman who has the eyes to foresee the person I am today, discrediting and contradicting the rest of the world, who told me I would be either in prison or dead by the age of 21. She is a caring woman who has loved me for me from the very beginning, not for what she could get from me, because I can assure you that I had nothing beneficial or productive to give when we met.

Jan sacrificed her time and energy to a lost and hopeless child who was full of pain and bitterness toward the world and everything in it because she could see his potential to become a man with something to offer. She willingly endured the growing pains of a boy as he matured and learned to become the man full of wisdom, knowledge, and power that she always knew was within.

Jan is an independent and self-sufficient woman who refuses to settle for less or accept mediocrity, no matter the circumstances, with or without the approval of others; a natural-born leader who understands the importance of being quick to hear and slow to speak; a silent but deadly opponent at the snap of a finger; an empowering and encouraging woman who always reminds me to use the negatives from my past to create a better future and tells me that the greatest way to silence the doubters and naysayers is simply to succeed.

Jan is a soldier, always hands-on, never sitting on the sidelines. She is a true representation of the support any real man needs to stay focused and continue to push forward through each phase of life. Jan says what she means and means what she says.

She loves and trusts God and is a true representation of who and what she believes in, even till her death.

Jan brings light to the dark, smiles to the sad, joy to the brokenhearted, love to the hurt, strength to the weak, and hope to the hopeless; to say she has a strong work ethic, excellent morals, great character, and a magnetic and cheerful attitude would be an understatement.

Jan is the most Christ-like of anyone I have ever encountered in my life, a true woman of God who is full of faith and walks what she talks!

Jan, I need you to know that I love you, I miss you, and I am eternally grateful for every investment you made into my life that has undisputedly played a major role in making me the man I am today.

I will always love you, Jan, and I will see you again.

Brian P. Lucas
BRIAN P. LUCAS

Dedication

I dedicate this book to every one of you who has invested your time and energy into reading it and is seriously interested in implementing the changes required to be the best you that you desire to be and to be all that God has ordained and sanctified you to be.

Congratulations on taking a step forward toward improvement for yourself and your family and allowing me to be a part of your journey.

I wish you the very best to truly succeed in all your endeavors, and I encourage you to keep reading books, learning new things, and exposing yourself to experiences that challenge you to make sacrifices and implement changes that ultimately promote elevation, growth, and development.

I strongly encourage you to use this time as an investment with the hopes of achieving a huge return. To do so, you will need to eliminate any distractions and make reading, studying, and comprehending each chapter of this book a priority.

Thank you for granting me permission to speak into your life. I assure you that I will be 100 percent real with you on all levels; I will be very blunt, holding nothing back and telling it just like it is through the duration of the book.

I look forward to your success as you take this journey one chapter at a time.

Walk in your Authority, Dominion, and Power

Brian P. Lucas
BRIAN P. LUCAS

Table of Contents

Lifetime Thanks v
Dedication vii
Foreword xi
Introduction xii
Chapter 1: The Garden 1
Chapter 2: Know Who You Are 15
Chapter 3: Rightful Position 25
Chapter 4: Jesus is NOT a Religion 37
Chapter 5: Religion is NOT Relationship 43
Chapter 6: Unequally Yoked and MANipulated 57
Chapter 7: Escape the Pig Pen 67
Appendix 83
Bonus Chapter: reDefine Thought 85
Conclusion 119
Why Jesus? 124
Salvation 125
About the Author 127

Foreword

There are journeys in life that can either strengthen or weaken the traveler. While the outcome is never certain, one of the most significant factors influencing it is the path taken.

A series of poor decisions — whether within or beyond the traveler's control — can deplete his ability to focus on others, increase the likelihood of future missteps, and ultimately lead to a life unintended and undesired.

That has not been Brian's fate.

Despite his challenging beginnings, God has seen fit to expand his capacity for wisdom, selflessness, and sound decision making.

As a result, Brian has built a life of purpose, one that reflects God's guidance and calling.

I have had the privilege of knowing Brian for over 20 years, and throughout that time, one thing has remained constant: God's hand on his life.

He has been blessed with wisdom, a heart for others, and a natural ability to lead. In many ways, he has been an example to me in all three areas.

His journey sets him apart from others who have walked similar paths, and because of that, he brings a unique perspective on what it truly means to walk in authority, dominion, and power.

I am confident that this book will inspire and equip you to do the same.

VON HAWTHORNE
COO Tru Treasury

Introduction

I can assure you that I am disclosing information in every chapter of this book that most people do not want you to know because it hinders their advantage and eliminates their control over you and your family.

Make it a point to go through each chapter with an open mind and an open heart, seeking revelation and confirmation. It may be difficult at times due to the brainwashing and conditioning of religion and the society we live in, but you must press forward towards the prize to reap the benefits of the Truth.

For many, it will be very challenging to accept the fact that you have more than likely been purposely lied to for most of your life by the ones closest to you.

Real freedom is only in Truth because it is the Truth that makes you free.

May God bless you with the eyes to see and the ears to hear the Truth over the lie as you read, study, and do your due diligence.

Matthew 18:11

For the Son of man [Jesus] is come to save that which was *lost*.

- Jesus is come to save that which was *lost*.
- Jesus is come to save you!

How can you be *lost* if you were never there?

People only know what they know. Satan's agenda is for you to never know and to keep you blinded from the Truth for as long as possible so that you will never really understand and *Know Who You Are*.

John 10:10

The thief cometh not, but for to steal, and to kill, and to destroy: [Jesus has] come that they might have life, and that they might have [life] more abundantly.

- Jesus is come that they might have *life* and that they may have *life* more abundantly.
- Jesus is come to give you *life*!
- Jesus is come that you might have *life* more abundantly!

Why do you need *life* if you are already alive?

Do not allow the enemy to steal your seeds of wisdom, knowledge, and understanding away from you.

You must eliminate all fear and doubt, and let God lead you.

As God told Joshua, I pray that you will be *strong* and of a *good courage* as you invest your time and energy into reading and learning the information provided.

Joshua 1:6

Be strong and of a good courage:

Joshua 1:7

Only be [you] strong and very courageous...

Joshua 1:9

Have not I commanded [you]?

Be strong and of good courage; be not afraid, neither be [you] dismayed: for the LORD [your] God is with [you wherever you go].

Joshua 1:8

This book of the law shall not depart out of [my] mouth; but [I] shalt meditate therein day and night, that [I] mayest observe to do according to all that is written therein: for then [I] shalt make [my] way prosperous, and then [I] shalt have good success.

Prosperity and good success belong to you when you are *speaking the Word*, *meditating on the Word*, and *acting on the Word*.

- Speak the Word: Talk like God.
- Meditate on the Word: Think like God.
- Act on the Word: Act like God.

As God told Joshua, I pray that this book will fall into this category for you and your family and all that make a choice to read it and that you will have a full understanding of why a *Back to the Garden* mentality and mindset is so important.

I pray that there is at least one thing in this book that causes the "a-ha moment" that sticks with you and your family for generations to come.

To living in your *Rightful Position* and original intent,

BRIAN P. LUCAS

BACK TO THE GARDEN

Chapter 1: The Garden

Let's begin with the beginning, shall we? And that is none other than the Book of Genesis.

It is extremely important that you understand exactly what takes place in *The Garden* so that you can begin to realize and truly *Know Who You Are*.

For you to be the real you and be all that God has equipped you to be, you must understand the original intent and your *Rightful Position*.

Genesis 1:26-28

[26] And God said, Let us make man in our image, after our likeness: and let them have dominion over the fish of the sea, and over the fowl of the air, and over the cattle, and over all the earth, and over every creeping thing that [creeps] upon the earth.

[27] So God created man in his own image, in the image of God created he him; male and female created he them.

[28] And God blessed them, and God said unto them, Be fruitful, and multiply, and replenish the earth, and subdue it: and have dominion over the fish of the sea, and over the fowl of the air, and over every living thing that [moves] upon earth.

So, your beginning starts with you being created by God in His image and likeness and Him blessing you and giving you the ability to *walk in your authority, dominion, and power* to rule the Earth.

Genesis 2:15-17

¹⁵ And the LORD God took [Adam], and put [Adam] into the Garden of Eden to dress it and to keep it.

¹⁶ And the LORD God commanded [Adam], saying, Of every tree of the Garden [you may] freely eat:

¹⁷ But of the tree of the knowledge of good and evil, [you] shalt not eat of it: for in the day that [you eat of the tree you] shalt surely die.

Here in these verses, we have the commandment from God of what is accessible, and the one thing that is not, as well as a full explanation of the penalty of *death*, which is the consequence for violating His command. God is a *righteous* God. God provided you with the *power of choice* from the very beginning, and Adam was given the choice to obey or disobey God's Word.

Genesis 2:7-9

⁷ And the LORD God formed man of the dust of the ground, and breathed into his nostrils the breath of life; and man became a living soul.

⁸ And the LORD God planted a Garden eastward in Eden; and there he put the man whom he had formed.

⁹ And out of the ground made the LORD God to grow every tree that is pleasant to the sight, and good for food; the tree of *Life* also in the midst of the Garden, and the tree of knowledge of good and evil.

The opportunity to choose *life* was always there from the beginning, which is why the Devil's goal then (and still today) is to *eliminate life* and make *death* look appealing in the process.

Satan wants to keep you <u>blinded, distracted, and lost!</u>

The very thing that we are all searching for is in the Garden, and it has been readily available the whole time. The enemy's goal is to make sure you choose *death* instead of *life*. Every day you are outside of the Garden, you are outside of your original intent and outside of your *Rightful Position*. Without the *life*, you are *walking, talking, breathing* **death** — nothing more and nothing less!

Genesis 2:16-17

[16] And the LORD God commanded [Adam], saying, Of every tree of the Garden [you may] freely eat:

[17] But of the tree of the knowledge of good and evil, [you] shalt not eat of it: for in the day that [you eat of the tree you] shalt surely die.

Here is a recap of the command that was given by God and the results for disobedience.

Genesis 3:1-3

[1] Now the serpent was more [sly, cunning, and crafty] than any beast of the field which the LORD God had made. And [the serpent] said unto [Eve], [Yes has] God said, [You] shall not eat of every tree of the Garden?

[2] And [Eve] said unto the serpent, We may eat of the fruit of the trees of the Garden:

[3] But of the fruit of the tree which is in the midst of the Garden, God [has] said, [You] shall not eat of [the tree], neither shall [you] touch it, [or else you] die.

Eve is now clearly explaining and demonstrating her *faith* in and *understanding* of the command that was given by God.

Genesis 3:4-5

⁴ And the serpent said unto [Eve, You] shall not surely die:

⁵ For God [does] know that in the day [you] eat [of the tree of knowledge of good and evil], then your eyes shall be opened, and [you] shall be as gods, knowing good and evil.

The serpent is now providing the *contradiction of the commandment and of God's Word*.

Genesis 3:6

And when [Eve] saw that the tree was good for food, and that it was pleasant to the eyes, and a tree to be desired to make one wise, she took of the fruit [of the tree], and did eat, and gave also unto [Adam (her husband) who was] with [Eve]; and [Adam] did eat.

Adam and Eve have now decided to put their *faith* in the *contradiction of the commandment and of God's Word*. Adam and Eve purposely and willfully violate God's commandment and choose to leave *life* to enter *death*, and this is the definition of **_LOST_**.

Genesis 3:7

And the eyes of [Adam and Eve] were opened, and [Adam and Eve] knew that they were naked; and [Adam and Eve] sewed fig leaves together, and made themselves aprons.

The first thing that contributed to Adam and Eve being *lost* was the *loss of identity*.

Genesis 3:8

And [Adam and Eve] heard the voice of God walking in the Garden in the cool of the day: and Adam and his wife [Eve] hid themselves from the presence of the LORD God amongst the trees of the Garden.

Adam and Eve are now attempting to hide from the LORD God, their Creator.

When you lose your identity, you no longer *Know Who You Are*, and you forget who you belong to and who created you in the first place. Only a *lost* person believes that it is possible to hide from God.

Genesis 3:9

And the LORD God called unto Adam, and said unto [Adam], Where [are you]?

The blunt and direct answer would be *lost*!

Genesis 3:10

And [Adam] said, I heard [your] voice in the Garden, and I was *afraid*, because I was naked; and I hid myself.

With the *loss of identity*, no longer being able to *Know Who You Are*, being outside the original intent and *Rightful Position*, ultimately comes ***FEAR!***

2 Timothy 1:7

For God [has] not given us the spirit of fear; but of power, and of love, and of a sound mind.

If God does not give the *spirit of fear*, then how can Adam and Eve *speak* the word "*afraid*"?

Fear eliminates your power, love, and a sound mind because these are the alternatives to illustrate what God did provide us versus what God never provided us.

When we disobey God, we put ourselves at a disadvantage and allow Satan to instill fear in us, which steals, kills, and destroys our blessing of authority, dominion, power, love, and a sound mind. In *fear*, we are *lost* in a demonic and Satanic spirit outside of the original intent and position that God placed us in.

Read Genesis 3:11-19

- No authority, dominion, or power
- Blame shifting
- Failure to take responsibility
- Failure to acknowledge wrongdoing
- Failure to admit and repent
- Loss of identity
- Fear
- Out of *Rightful Position*
- *Lost*

Read Genesis 3:22-24

- Removal from *Life* for choosing *Death*
- *Lost*

Now, let me make one huge misconception and religious man-made idea very clear: neither Eve nor the serpent ever lied. Everything Eve said to the serpent was true, and everything the serpent said to Eve was true.

There is so much erroneous non-biblical teaching surrounding this subject. They try their very best to force verses to fit their narratives, but everything the serpent told Eve was true.

Genesis 3:1

Now the serpent was more [sly, cunning, and crafty] than any beast of the field which the LORD God had made. And [the serpent] said unto [Eve], [Yes has] God said, [You] shall not eat of every tree of the Garden?

Notice that this is a question to engage Eve into the conversation — not a statement. It is a very sly, cunning, and crafty way to engage, by asking a question he already knows the answer to, but at no point in this conversation does the serpent lie.

Genesis 3:4

And the serpent said unto [Eve, You] shall not surely die:

They did not physically die, so this is true, too.

Genesis 3:5

For God [does] know that in the day [you] eat [of the tree of knowledge of good and evil], then your eyes shall be opened, and [you] shall be as gods, knowing good and evil.

As the serpent states, this is 100% true.

Genesis 3:22

And the LORD God said, Behold [Adam and Eve] is become as one of us, to know good and evil: and now, [or else they put forth their hands], and take also of the Tree of Life, and eat, and live for ever:

God is now stating and repeating exactly what the serpent told Eve, so this is also true.

Now, let's address the non-biblical attack the church, religion, and the traditions of men have lined out for Eve. They always claim that Eve was lying or making stuff up in her conversation with the serpent, and this could not be further from the Truth.

Everything Eve told the serpent was the Truth.

Genesis 3:2

And [Eve] said unto the serpent, We may eat of the fruit of the trees of the Garden:

This is 100% Truth.

Genesis 3:3

But of the fruit of the tree which is in the midst of the Garden, God [has] said, [You] shall not eat of [the tree], neither shall [you] touch it, [or else you] die.

And this also must be 100% Truth.

Now, here is where all the make-believe and storytelling comes into play.

People think that just because there is no encounter or specific verse that we can read that highlights a command to "touch it" that Eve is not being truthful. Just because we are not able to read what God specifically told Adam and Eve does not mean that it did not happen. On the contrary, because it is written that Eve said God said it, it is so much easier to conclude that, at one point or another, God said it.

Genesis 2:16-17

[16] And the LORD God commanded [Adam], saying, Of every tree of the Garden [you may] freely eat:

[17] But of the tree of the knowledge of good and evil, [you] shalt not eat of it: for in the day that [you eat of the tree you] shalt surely die.

We read these verses, and because it does not say "neither shall you touch it," we just decide to write Eve off as a liar, and all this other foolishness we read and hear preached about the subject.

Genesis 3:2-3

[2] And [Eve] said unto the serpent, We may eat of the fruit of the trees of the Garden:

[3] But of the fruit of the tree which is in the midst of the Garden, God [has] said, [You] shall not eat of [the tree], neither shall [you] touch it, [or else you] die.

Notice the phrase "God has said."

Eve is speaking truthfully in the authority and dominion that she was given by God, and she clearly states "God hath said." Eve did not just make this up and pull it out of the sky, just like the serpent did not make anything up when he spoke. Both Eve and the serpent knew full well what they were saying and doing in the process of this conversation.

Eve is repeating what she was told and what she heard whether it was directly from God Himself or from Adam telling her that God said it. Either way, *God said it!*

How can I be so sure?

Simple. Adam and Eve were made in perfection and righteousness in the image and likeness of God.

Genesis 1:26-27

[26] And God said, Let us make man in our image, after our likeness: and let them have dominion over the fish of the sea, and over the fowl of the air, and over the cattle, and over all the earth, and over every creeping thing that [creeps] upon the earth.

[27] So God created man in his own image, in the image of God created he him male and female created he them.

How exactly is it that Eve can lie or make up extra stuff at this point?

It is silly simple — she can't!

At this point, Eve doesn't even know good and evil, she only knows God. Eve only knows perfection and righteousness, and she is as much like God as she could ever be outside of the knowledge of good and evil.

If you don't even know evil, then you can't do it.

Romans 10:17

So then faith [comes] by hearing, and hearing by the Word of God.

Faith in something comes by hearing something — Faith Comes By Hearing.

Genesis 3:2-3

² And [Eve] said unto the serpent, We may eat of the fruit of the trees of the Garden:

³ But of the fruit of the tree which is in the midst of the Garden, God [has] said, [You] shall not eat of [the tree], neither shall [you] touch it, [or else you] die.

Eve shows you clearly who and what her *faith* is in when she responds to the serpent. She is repeating what she heard, either directly from God or from what Adam told her God said. Either way, it is Truth because there is no lie in God.

Eve is operating in the image and likeness of God, in perfection and righteousness, until she disobeys the command of God and eats the fruit of the tree of the knowledge of good and evil in Verse 6.

Genesis 3:6

And when [Eve] saw that the tree was good for food, and that it was pleasant to the eyes, and a tree to be desired to make one wise, she took of the fruit [of the tree], and did eat, and gave also unto [Adam (her husband) who was] with [Eve]; and [Adam] did eat.

Before Verse 6, Eve is not capable of doing anything evil, simply because for her up to this point, evil does not exist. Of course, evil has always existed, but for Eve in this moment, before she eats the fruit in disobedience, it does not exist for her because she has no knowledge of it.

This is why Satan's strategy and tactic was to entice Eve to eat the fruit from the tree of the knowledge of good and evil in the first place, so that evil or the Devil could enter by choice and not by force.

This works the same way in reverse. God provides you with a choice, just like He did with Adam and Eve, or else it wouldn't really be fair or righteous.

We always have a choice!

2 Timothy 2:15

Study to [show yourself] approved to God, a workman that [needs] not to be ashamed, rightly dividing the Word of Truth.

This is why it is so important that you read your Bible and build a relationship with God for yourself. Let the Holy Spirit reveal and confirm not man, religion, traditions, rules, and regulations.

God is your only true Source!

And I am not exempt. Do not just take what I say/write as truth. Go to your Bible, seek God, ask for revelation, and try the Spirit and see for yourself.

I, unlike many others, do not write books to be seen, for accolades or recognition. I write in obedience to do what God has told me to do, not to entertain or appease.

I am writing to convict, resonate, encourage, empower, reveal, confirm, and ultimately bring about elevation, growth, and development that pushes the buttons inside of you to motivate a change that gives you the courage to walk in Truth as a bright light amidst darkness and fulfill *Kingdom Purpose*.

If only one person gets it, then I have done my duty and fulfilled my assignment.

Every day we wake up, we are on assignment and have a purpose to fulfill. This is true for all of us, whether it be for good or evil. We are all contributing factors either way. We must make a choice and decide which side of the Garden we want to be in, or better yet, if we want to be in the Garden or forced outside of it like Adam and Eve. We are all outside of the Garden until we find out who we are and who we belong to.

The World's System and the demonic agenda promote and advertise a great life outside of the Garden, but anything outside of the Garden can only emulate and empower _death_ because it is the only remaining option outside of God.

There is no _life_ outside of the _Creator of Life_. God is the Potter, and we are the clay; without the Potter, the clay is *nothing*, has no life, and is _dead_.

There is a lot of talk about being lost, getting saved, eternal life, and being born again, but what does that even mean?

- How am I lost?
- What must I be saved from?
- What is eternal life?
- How can one be born again?

Religion has an absolute field day with these questions and provides us with so many answers that we can all find something that resonates and meets our desires. Then we religiously focus on that desire in hopes that it will bring us the peace and understanding that we are desperately searching for.

The problem is that religion does not bring peace and understanding. It usually brings a temporal fulfillment, which is bluntly foolishness that has no bearing on the Truth.

The lie is always easier to sell. It feels better, so it is easier to accept.

How many years have you wasted believing in a partial truth or even a blatant lie?

The father of lies is in the church building, and he is making the church a den of thieves! Satan has turned the house of prayer into a place of entertainment, with every worldly distraction on the menu standing right behind the pulpit.

The selfish and the greedy have taken the message of hope and have used it to manipulate and control you rather than enlighten you and make you free. They have taken the wisdom and knowledge of salvation and life and perverted it so that people remain *lost*, which is the ultimate <u>*death*</u>, both during life and after — *The Walking Dead!*

<u>You must Know Who You Are!</u>

Notes:

Chapter 2: Know Who You Are

You were created for a purpose. Your assignment to complete every day that you wake up is to benefit and encourage someone else.

How can you successfully do this if you do not *Know Who You Are?*

You have been gifted and anointed to be a light that shines in darkness to encourage and empower others to see the truth amid lies.

Blinded eyes must see, and deaf ears must hear. You have been chosen and ordained and sanctified to make a difference in the lives of those that need help to see and hear that Jesus is the key to every door, the solution to every problem, and the answer to every question.

We must step out of this World's System and get *Back to the Garden* mentality and mindset that best illustrates who we really are. God has given us authority, dominion, and power, and it's time that we take our rightful place and walk in it.

Life is full of choices, and we must be cognizant of the decisions we make. Each one is either beneficial and productive or detrimental and destructive to our well-being.

Sometimes what seems right has ill intent and the wrong motive. This is another reason we must be aware and intentional in building a real relationship with our Father God.

The opposition is always present and providing you with alternatives, with the hope that he can make the contradiction of God's Word more intriguing than the Word of God and the power that comes from it. Every day you are presented with another option, just like Adam and Eve in the Garden.

The enemy will present it with the best ribbons and bows, packaged to meet and exceed your desires, but it is all a facade to distract you from the truth about yourself and deter you from fulfilling your God-Given Purpose. It looks, sounds, smells, tastes, and feels good, but it is not good for you and is the lie of all lies coming from the father of lies. Any promise to empower you to be more than what God has already provided and equipped is nothing more than a purposeful lie. It is a fictitious choice that leads you nowhere fast. The created will never outperform the Creator. It is impossible!

Do not be fooled by the hype and by what things look like in the natural on the surface. I can assure you the grass is never greener on the other side of God's Word and God's Will for your life. Nothing and no one will ever be able to do for you like God will. To invest time and energy into the opposition is just plain outright foolish and really makes no sense at all. God is All, and All is God, and outside of God, there is *NOTHING!*

This is not hard to understand if we are rational and honest with ourselves and take time to think about it with due diligence and an open mind, without the distractions of the opposition.

People invest more time and energy into the lies. This is why most of our theology and so-called truth is nothing more than another lie introduced and advertised by the liar in the Garden. For one to think or believe that they could ever be more than what God created them to be is just foolishness, but this is exactly where we are today. People really preach and teach this fictitious lifestyle and use the Bible and God's Word to do it, and because most people do not read their Bible for themselves, or study to show themselves approved, or rightly divide the Word of Truth, they fall right into this manipulating ditch full of lies.

Look around the world — are things getting better?

Right is wrong and wrong is right, and we have become accepting of anything, even the very things we completely disagree with. Why is that? How did we get here?

Conditioning and the decision to compromise!

The ones who used to expose wrongdoing and malicious ungodly behavior are now sitting right next to, promoting, and benefiting from the people they once condemned. In addition, they have agreed to manipulate you and keep you under control of the lies in the process. They are no different from the very people Jesus confronted and condemned for deceiving God's people — the exact same thing is happening today. They want to remain in power and benefit from the government and the powers that be, so they use their position with the facade of godliness and hustle, trick, and trap God's people with religion, rules, regulations, and traditions of men to keep them enslaved to the World's System for their own personal benefit and gain.

The hireling does not care for nor respect the flock and is just looking to get what they can for self. This is most church leaders and religious leaders today. They keep you blinded, deaf, broke, and enslaved while they remain in power and get rich on the backs of God's people.

When you do not *Know Who You Are*, you are easily controlled and taken advantage of. The World's System wants to keep you outside of the Garden mentality and mindset because they know that if you ever realize who you truly are, they will no longer have this power and control over you and your family, and you will become a threat to the world's agenda.

The opposition does not attack his own, nor will he invest time and energy into those who already don't know, because they are simply no threat to him. You may not fully understand the power of knowledge — and more so, the power of knowledge that is utilized — but this is pertinent for both you and your family. The more you know, the more of a threat you become. This is why keeping you as ignorant as they can is their ultimate weapon and goal.

I assure you that they do not want you to know what is being provided to you right now in this book. Truth shines a bright light on darkness and exposes the hidden agendas, which makes it more challenging for them to take advantage of you and your family. We must realize that everything we need in this life begins in the Garden with Adam and Eve. God's Word is powerful and alive and will fulfill what has been spoken and has already fulfilled it. Remember, the spiritual goes before the natural, and we are always playing catch up in the natural to what has already been done in the spiritual. You are already blessed!

If you pay attention, you will realize the power you have as a speaking spirit to call those things that are not as though they are. You must *Know Who You Are* and the power that God has placed within you. Nothing and no one can take God's place in your life.

This is not religion I speak of. This is a real relationship with the Creator of All Things.

Religion is not Relationship!

People do not want to admit that their whole lives have been man-made religious, denominational, and theological experiences that holds no true value or comparison to a relationship with God.

We have been conditioned to believe that attending meetings, paying tithes and offerings, praying theatrical prayers, high fiving our neighbors, running around the building, doing slave dances, repeating things we don't even believe, and carrying around the unread Bible, is a form of a relationship, and this could not be further from the truth. The Bible tells us clearly that people are destroyed and perish due to the lack of knowledge, and the lack of knowledge also includes the lack of relationship.

You must make it a point to know who your Father God is for yourself. You will never know your true value or purpose if you don't know your Source, the Creator of All Things.

Why do you think man in the natural (which is a representation of the Father) is always under attack?

Why is the man and the head of the home always pushed, pressed, and tested to empower failure in his life and in his home?

Think about it. Why is there this demand suddenly for the effeminate man?

Why does the man always seem to be under attack for simply being a man?

Why is the World's System marketing and advertising and shoving down our throats soft men who do not portray masculinity?

Why are we suddenly confused about the simplicity of him, his, and he?

Where does this foolishness come from, and why do the leaders and those with so-called authority promote it and defend it?

How is it that the heterosexual man is now the minority and is looked down upon in society? How did we get here?

Under the guise of rights and freedoms and equality, we now have a society that accepts what was once the abnormal and purposely attacks the normal by shoving the abnormal down our throats. They attempt to force acceptance by banishing anyone who does not agree or comply with their agenda.

So, they promote freedom and equality for the abnormal but say screw those of you who are normal. Get on board with the abnormal or be isolated. Forget about God, the Bible, morals, ethics, values, and all you feel is right, and bow down to what we are telling you is right.

How is this equality?

They have a choice, but we do not. How is this fair or right in anyone's eyes?

If one does not agree with the abnormal or speaks against it, then it is considered a hate crime, but if someone does not like another person because of the color of their skin and discriminates, then it is considered normal? How did we get here?

Does one have to like another if they are from a different culture or background and be accepting of their ways? Then how is it that the abnormal must be accepted?

ANYTHING THAT ELIMINATES YOUR CHOICE IS DEMONIC!!!

In the Garden, God provided Adam and Eve with the power of choice, and they were able to decide whether they wanted to obey and follow God's Word or not.

Who are we now to attempt to defy the power of choice and force decisions upon people when God gave them the power and authority to choose for themselves?

Now, everyone reading this will be able to apply this to various things for themselves, which is why I am purposely being vague in my writing. It means many different things for many different people, so it is wise to write accordingly. However, I want to be very clear as far as I am concerned so it is not confused: it is not my intention to divide. If it is Bible, I am in agreement, and if it is not Bible, then I am not in agreement.

Basically, don't just throw me into your subject matter and assume I agree or disagree because I may or may not depending on what God reveals to me through His Word.

I am not here to judge or condemn, only to deliver the Word that God has given me. I stay in my lane and let God do what God does.

Chaos, confusion, and fear enters when we are out of position.

- A man must be a man and take his *Rightful Position* as a Man.
- A woman must be a woman and take her *Rightful Position* as a Woman.

The man specifically is under attack to eliminate the God-given order and empower chaos, confusion, and fear. To remove the man is to remove the head, and to remove the head is to remove the direction and order that was given by God, the Creator. Spiritually, naturally, scientifically, biblically, and logically, this has proven to be the case. This is why the agenda must attack men from every angle, to keep them out of their God-given rights of authority, dominion, and power that God gave Man in the Garden.

The woman is ordained and sanctified by God to be the helpmeet to the man, to encourage and empower him to be all that God has called him to be. However, the World's System and society has purposely and maliciously promoted, marketed, and advertised the role of a woman to override and supersede the man, and in many cases to attempt to play the role of the man outside of her God-given position, which is not God's original intent.

The enemy does not want you to walk in your God-given authority, so he provides you with alternatives to keep you blinded and distracted. The Devil hates you because you remind him of the same God that stripped him of his power. However, instead of being a reflection and representation of God, we allow the Devil to mock God through our lack of knowledge, lack of relationship, and failure to take our *Rightful Position*.

Men and Women simply must do better in every area.

Make it a point to *Know Who You Are!*

Notes:

Notes:

Chapter 3: Rightful Position

Men must be men, and women must be women. Men and Women must be in position to play out and fulfill the God-given role they have been ordained and sanctified to fulfill.

The Devil is your enemy, and his job is to keep you outside of the will and the original intent of God. Satan creates options to go against the Word of God, which take you out of position.

The man's role and the woman's role are clear. We do not need man-made interpretations and changed verbiage to understand the God-given rules that have been assigned.

Every time man attempts to go outside of the Word, or the original intent, chaos follows!

We will never be successful going against the Word and the direction of God!

The trick and the trap of the enemy is to keep you distracted with the alternatives and the illusion of a choice outside of God's Will, with the hope that the alternative will be better than the plan that God has already assigned you.

God is the Potter, and we are the clay. No choice outside of the Potter will be beneficial to the clay — it is *impossible!*

God is almighty and all powerful, and He has already set in motion what we need to succeed, but man gets in the way with foolishness, trying to outperform the Creator of All Things.

Man's ways and foolishness will never be able to coincide with the Truth, the original intent, and the ultimate Will of God. God is above all. His thoughts are not our thoughts, and His ways are above our ways. We are not in any way, shape, or form able to compare to the greatness of God. Even the opposition was created by God. You cannot win or succeed without the power of God on your side; no matter which way you decide to go, God is the Creator of all.

Without God, we are absolutely nothing!

The reverence of God is the beginning of wisdom and knowledge, so one cannot be considered wise or knowledgeable without coming to the realization that God is the *I AM THAT I AM*, and all things belong to Him. The Earth is the Lord's and the fullness thereof, and all that dwells therein is the Lord's, and this includes you.

You are fearfully and wonderfully made, and there is only one you. There is no duplicate; you are the original, and there is no other. You are made in the image and likeness of God your Creator, and you were made in perfection with authenticity. Any changes, alterations, and ideas to reconstruct what God formed and made are clearly disrespectful to the Creator and the original intent.

How does the clay tell the Potter that the Potter is wrong?

Clay does not talk; it just molds into what the Potter desires!

This *New World Order* and this new way of living to fulfill the *Agenda of Depopulation* must be exposed. The truth must be disclosed so we can reach those who know deep down that something about this whole "woke" movement is artificial, to say the least.

Effeminate Men with *Superhero Women* and no reproduction is not the original intent and plan of God! Men with men and Women with women cannot and will never reproduce and replenish the Earth as commanded.

Only a person who has no knowledge of God can really believe that the Earth will run out of resources because there are too many people on the planet for the Earth to sustain.

This theory and idea are absolutely foolish!

On one hand, they tell us that the Earth is billions of years old, and on the other hand, they say we are suddenly running out of resources, global warming is destroying the planet, and the world is falling apart because of man and overpopulation.

This theory is contradictive and hypocritical, to say the least. It is outright foolishness. When you know there is a God, it simply does not matter. It is not the universe or any silly secret that created all things. God is your Creator and Provider — *not* the Earth or the universe!

Don't fall into the trap of worshipping the created. Worship the Creator! God is the only entity to be worshipped: Father, Son, and Spirit — that's it!

None of this other foolishness will suffice in the end. Do not make a god out of something God created! That makes no sense at all!

Why would you worship anything that was created by the Creator?

Why do you think God is a jealous God?

God created the cow and then created us. God gave us authority and dominion over the cow, but then we submit that authority and dominion over to the cow and worship the cow that we were given authority over. How does this make sense?

God created rocks and trees and then gifted us to build with the rocks and trees, and what do we do with this God-given gift? We build statues to worship. Does that make sense?

As intelligent as we proclaim and portray ourselves to be, we really do some very silly and stupid things that make no sense at all!

God will not be mocked, yet we sure try His patience with some of the most disrespectful imaginations of wickedness — then we wonder why our lives suck so badly. Stop giving your honor, praise, and worship to things that are created by the Creator and simply give your honor, praise, and worship to the Creator!

This is not difficult to understand. This is very simple and basic common sense for anyone who just takes a little time to think for themselves and stop allowing the foolishness of man to cloud their judgment.

God is almighty and powerful. Worship God, not the stuff God created and provided! God is above all, and Him and only Him shall we serve. There are no ifs, ands, or buts in that statement. It is not debatable or dependent on how you feel. God and only God is to be worshipped and served.

Do not be tricked and fooled by the man-made hype and all the purposeful distractions intended to steer you away from the Truth.

Everything that shines isn't gold — sometimes it's copper!

Both serve purposes and in their own rights are beneficial, but only one is gold. Both are created by God, so neither should be served, worshipped, or put above the Creator and the Source of all things.

We are so easily distracted by things, and it's usually by things that don't really matter and will not contribute to a better life.

God is the Creator of all and has equipped you with all that you need to survive and thrive. Do not sleep on this truth. All you need is the Source of all things. *God is all you need!*

- The universe cannot help you.
- Secrets of foolishness will not help you.
- Cows, trees, and rocks will not suffice.
- Gold, statues, and the traditions of men won't help you.
- Religion or any other man-made doctrine can't help you.

Only the Creator and the Source of life will provide you with what you need to live a great life, for *life* is in Him!

What looks, sounds, tastes, smells, and feels good is not necessarily good for you. Just because something seems good does not mean it is right or the best thing for you.

If you are at a point in your life where you are seeking and searching for Truth, and you desperately and wholeheartedly want to fill the void and the emptiness that you feel inside, then what you need is the Truth — not more bells and whistles or fairytales and make-believe. If you are searching for Truth, then you simply need the Truth and nothing but the Truth.

Your God, your Creator, your Source, and your Father provides you the Truth, and that Truth is in the name above every name where every knee shall bow, and every tongue shall confess that *Jesus is Lord!*

Jesus is the Truth that you are seeking!

Nothing and nobody else will suffice. Jesus is the Way, the Truth, and the Life, and no one comes to God the Father but in, by, and through Jesus. Jesus is the answer you are seeking.

Read it over and over again, and speak it over and over again until it begins to marinate and resonate within. You are nothing without Jesus, and you can do nothing without Jesus.

- **Jesus is the *Way*.**
- Jesus is the only *Way* to *Truth* because He is the *Truth*.
- **Jesus is the *Truth*.**
- Jesus is the only *Way* to *Life* because He is the *Life*.
- ***Jesus is the Life.***

This is the order and the original intent that God set in place, and it is perfect in its entirety. God does not need man's help with the outline and the order that has already been set in place. God needs man to simply get in the position that was originally intended from the beginning. He requires and demands man's obedience and reverence. God really doesn't need our worldly-minded input. He requires your spiritual revelation and worship, which can only come from your true self. This means you must *Know Who You Are* to be what you have been ordained and sanctified to be.

The most detrimental feeling in life is to not Know Who You Are!

We spend so much time seeking fulfillment and trying to position ourselves in this world to fit in, not really understanding that was never the original intent or plan that God has for us.

Rightful Position

You were instructed and commanded to subdue the Earth with authority and dominion, not to fit into the way of it. You are built to command and direct with authority and dominion by the Power of God within you, but if you do not *Know Who You Are*, you will never take your *Rightful Position* in this world.

You are in this world but not of this world. This simply means that you do not belong to the World's System. You are here on assignment to fulfill purpose, not to be enslaved to the ways of the world and the traditions of men.

Religion is a destroyer of Truth and relationship and creates unnecessary distractions to keep you focused on the things that hinder you from knowing who you truly are.

You have been given authority, dominion, and power to subdue the Earth just like Adam and Eve. The enemy still provides the same contradicting alternative to steal your identity, position, and God-given power away from you. When you are sidetracked and distracted, it is easy to take you out of your *Rightful Position*.

When we are out of position, we are outside of the original intent. This is what causes us to feel this emptiness and void on the inside, which makes us feel like something is missing.

We then go out of our way to try to fill this void on our own, in our own power and our own might, and it never seems to work out the way we hoped for in the end. Outside of God and outside of Truth, it never will.

You cannot look in the mirror and be mad, upset, or angry with the mirror about the reflection you see. It is not the mirror (which only does the reflecting), it is you who empowers the reflection the mirror provides. If you don't like what you see, don't blame the mirror, confront the man you see in the mirror.

You must take responsibility for your own actions. No one in this world of this world will ever be able to do more for you than you can do for yourself. You are your own best friend, and you are your own worst enemy.

Do not allow the enemy to trick you into believing that the world owes you something. Do not allow yourself to be blinded by the TRAP mentality and mindset. This world and its system are full of blame shifters who never want to admit to their own failures and wrongdoings. Instead of taking responsibility for their actions, they find others to point the finger at and place blame on them.

You will never change for the better if every problem or challenge you face is always someone else's fault. I have been in this horrible position myself, and I write from a place of experience. This is not a place you want to stay because in this position there is no beneficial or productive change.

When we are outside of our *Rightful Position*, we make ourselves easy targets for the Devil to manipulate us and keep us trapped. The World's System has brainwashed and conditioned us to be accepting of the very things that cause us hurt, harm, and pain. We are so naive that we let that same system dictate and provide us with the remedy and the relief for the pain that it is causing.

How does this make sense?

We accept the antidote for the hurt from the same system that initiated the hurt in the first place.

I know it is difficult for people to accept the fact that they are brainwashed, but the Truth is the Truth whether people like it and accept it or not. The Truth always hurts before it helps, and it is the Truth and only the Truth that makes you free. When you are free, you are free indeed.

Outside of the Truth is only the lie. Living a lie will never bring you happiness.

How can one be happy with oneself if the life they are currently living is one big lie?

I cannot write it enough — *You Must Know Who You Are!*

Break free from the World's System and get back in your *Rightful Position* and begin to live the life that God ordained and sanctified you to live.

Before you were here, God knew you. He has already equipped you with every gift you need to be successful in this life. Again, if you are still here then, you are on assignment, and you still have purpose to fulfill. You are not here for nothing. You are not here just to take up space. You are definitely not here to be the Devil's punching bag and to go through all the hurt, pain, and challenges of life. This is not God's original intent, nor is it your *Rightful Position*.

Start thinking for yourself, and stop allowing the World's System to define you. Make a choice to break away from the TRAP. *Get off the wheel* that rotates in a circular motion but goes absolutely nowhere fast. *Cut the strings* from the puppet master, become your own person, and get back in your *Rightful Position*.

If you have ever traveled by plane, then you are aware of the five-minute speech before every flight. One of the most important parts of this speech is the reminder to *put on your own mask first* in case of an emergency. Do not attempt to help others until you have properly secured self-first.

This is such a powerful representation of life. Within this mask is the oxygen you need to be able to breathe. If I spend my time trying to put this mask on everyone else, but I have not secured my own, then I am sacrificing myself and my well-being unnecessarily. This is the way most people live their lives.

When we allow the World's System to dictate who we are, we are putting the mask on that system and allowing that system to define us. Meanwhile, we need oxygen for ourselves because we do not know who we are. The enemy is crafty. Satan will keep you distracted with all the foolishness of life to make sure you are always putting on the World's System's mask and not your own, which leaves you suffocating and sacrificing yourself daily.

Every day you spend outside of God, the original intent, and your *Rightful Position*, you are gasping for the oxygen you need to survive because you are not putting on your own mask first.

How can you be helpful to someone else if you do not help yourself first? *You can't!*

It is a facade and a fake reality to keep you blinded from the Truth.

Religion, denominations, rules, regulations, and the traditions of men are all distractions that keep you putting on everyone else's mask instead of your own.

- *Religion is NOT a Relationship.*
- *Religion is NOT the Kingdom.*

Religion does not have you putting on your own mask first; it has you attempting to put on everyone else's while you suffer and can barely breathe in the process. This is why so many are hurting and unhappy with life — because they lack the "oxygen" required to function properly and are too focused on the purposeful distractions of Satan.

You must put your own mask on first!

- *Know Who You Are*
- *Know Who You Belong to*
- *Know What You Stand For*
- *Know Your Purpose*
- *Know Your Truth*

You must walk in the authority, dominion, and power that God has placed within you. Seek ye first the *Kingdom of God* and *God's righteousness*, and get back to the original intent in your *Rightful Position.*

Notes:

Chapter 4: Jesus is NOT a Religion

The way of the world is only death, and there is no life in it outside of God the Father, Jesus the Christ, and the Holy Spirit.

You will never find peace, love, and joy outside of your Creator. All that you search for is in Him. You cannot supplement God with anyone or anything else; it will never suffice. God is All, and All is God.

You need Truth to prosper, and the lie only brings about more death. Satan is the enemy and the opposition to your successful life, and the Devil only promotes the contradiction. Keep in mind: the Devil was created by the same God that created you.

How can evil created by God ever defeat God? Think about it.

Satan has no hope in ever defeating God; however, he can focus on you and defeat you. This is why you must be full of the armor of God to protect you and your family from the daily attacks of the Devil to keep you enslaved and trapped in the lie.

Truth makes you free, and only Truth will give you the power you need to overcome the tricks and schemes of the enemy.

The World's System is so fake and phony, but we put all our eggs in the world's basket and just hope for the best, which is impossible to receive outside of God.

Light will always overcome darkness, and Truth will always eliminate the lie. Real is Real, and Fake is Fake. God is the *only* Source. God is all you need. Don't get caught up with the fairytales of life — outside of God, you are absolutely *nothing!*

God provides you the *Way*, the *Truth*, and the *Life*. Outside of God is only death and more death.

The world mentality and mindset belong to the walking dead, with ears closed and eyes wide shut. Death eliminates spiritual sight and the ears to hear Truth over the lie. Jesus is the Truth, and Satan is the lie.

Choose you this day whom you will serve. You cannot serve two masters. You will either love the one and despise the other, or despise the one and love the other.

God is almighty and all powerful and the Creator of Heaven and Earth and all that dwell therein.

How do we not trust Him to be the *only* choice worth choosing?

Outside of God, there is nothing beneficial or productive for you or your family.

How is this difficult to understand?

When one plus one equals two, it is always two. Numbers never lie; only silly people do.

God is so amazing that even Satan must use His playbook to succeed in your life. The Devil is the creator of *nothing!* He is a thief who comes to steal, kill, and destroy.

Pay attention to your surroundings, and you will see Satan in all things produced by the World's System.

Unfortunately, this includes religion and the churches with their thousands of denominations that can't get along or agree on even the most simple things written in the Bible for all to read.

Religion is a destroyer because it only causes confusion and division, and neither of these are biblically accurate nor Godly by any means.

God is *not* the author of confusion. God is the best definition of *unity*, which is the opposition of division.

God never promised you or positioned you for religion. Religion is a man-made attempt to be God, but there is only one God.

What did the serpent tell Eve in the Garden to entice her to eat the fruit? "You will be like gods." This is the same deceptive tactic Satan uses on all of us today in the form of religion!

Please do not take this lightly or push this out of your mind. Really think about it for yourself. I am only throwing out the seed; it's up to you which ground you allow the seed to fall upon.

For those of you reading who are religious:

- How is that working out for you and your family?
- Are you happy?
- Do you have joy?
- Are you fulfilled and at your best?
- Are you satisfied with the results thus far?
- Is religion a winning scenario for you?

No, it's not, because religion is a facade and nothing more than a distraction to keep you blind, deaf, enslaved, and broken.

There is no life in religion!

God sent Jesus to give you life and life more abundantly. Jesus is the answer.

Like numbers never lie, Jesus never lies. But religion, which was conjured up by Satan, is nothing but lies, just like the history books they give children at school.

Religion is just another tool they use to brainwash and condition us to remain slaves to the World's System and keep us trapped from thinking for ourselves.

Your freedom is in Truth! Truth is the *only* thing that truly makes you free!

This is why Satan's agenda is to keep you as far away from the Truth as possible. Satan is the father of lies, and the World's System is orchestrated by Satan.

So, what does that tell you?

Every day, Satan is planting seeds by way of your natural senses. What you see, hear, smell, taste, and feel in the natural is constantly under attack by the enemy, and most have no clue that religion is a tool Satan utilizes to destroy us.

Again, there is no life in religion!

You must break away from the distraction, which only causes division, and begin to seek God for yourself. You do not need man or sprinkles of water to reach God; what you need is Jesus because He is the one and only way to God the Father. There are no ifs, ands, or buts in that statement! "One and only way" is so simple; it is impossible to be confused or to get lost when there is only one direction required and provided.

But what does religion do with this one and only way? It provides you with thousands of ways, and we wonder why it does not work. It is nothing more than a purposeful Satanic distraction to keep you lost and outside of the Truth.

Religion attempts to fulfill a role that only Jesus can fulfill, and He has already fulfilled it. People spend their time and energy focused on trying to be gods just like Adam and Eve did in the Garden, but the closest to God you will ever be is by simply accepting the Word that was provided, which is Jesus.

Religion is no different from the enticing offer the serpent made Eve to get her to partake of the fruit from the Tree of the Knowledge of Good and Evil. Religion is a ridiculous and unnecessary facade that entices you to attempt to be what you already are in, by, and through Jesus.

Jesus is NOT a Religion!

Adam and Eve were as close to God as they could ever be before they ate the fruit. Religion is just like the fruit of the tree. Seek a relationship, *not* the fruit.

Get *Back to the Garden* and back to the mentality and mindset of the original intent. Take back your *Rightful Position*, which God gave you before the disobedience and sin entered.

Be purpose on purpose to fulfill purpose!

Notes:

Chapter 5: Religion is NOT Relationship

There is no life outside of Jesus! You cannot get to God without Jesus, and you cannot get to Jesus without the Holy Spirit.

The Father, Son, and the Spirit are all one and the same. You cannot have one without the other, and that shoots holes through many religions and ungodly traditions of men.

Respectfully, it is a lot easier to believe in a Santa Claus and an Easter Bunny that lays eggs than most of this foolishness they are trying to shove down our throats as Truth.

Remember, it's the same people who made this foolishness up that created religion, and religion is nothing more than a substitute for a *relationship* with God.

They know that if they preach and teach *relationship*, then Truth is coming, which means you will no longer need them. That is and has always been the problem.

<u>They Do Not Want to Lose Their Control Over You!</u>

Having your own *relationship* with God and being able to think for yourself is a problem for those who want to keep you inside their special boxes.

- If you do not *Know Who You Are*, <u>You are Lost!</u>
- If you do not *Know Who You Belong To*, <u>You are Lost!</u>
- If you do not *Know Where You Come From*, <u>You are Lost!</u>
- If you do not *Know the Original Intent*, <u>You are Lost!</u>

If you have not _confessed_ with your mouth that Jesus Christ is Lord and _believed_ in your heart that God raised Jesus from the dead, You are Lost!

The wonderful thing is that you do not have to be. And let me be clear, even a person who has accepted Jesus and is saved can still be lost if they have not found their way back home yet. They are saved to go to Heaven and escape Hell, but here in this world and in this World's System, they are still very much lost.

I cannot express to you enough that it is the right here and the right now that makes the most impact on the lives of others. Religion teaches you to get saved to go to Heaven, and this misses the whole point of your purpose and your daily assignment.

If going to Heaven is the most important factor, then why doesn't God just take us to Heaven after we accept salvation?

Think about it! If the whole point is to go to Heaven, why is it prolonged?

Ask your religious leaders to explain this and make it make sense.

Good luck — it makes no sense at all. Why?

Because going to Heaven is not the purpose. One day you may go, and that is great, but what are you going to do while you are here?

This is the most important aspect of it all. If you are wired to only think about going to Heaven, then you are missing the most important point of why you were put here to begin with.

You are not here for yourself. You are here for others, and I am not talking about the religious people who are taking advantage of you and using God's Word to do it.

You have a purpose to fulfill if you are still here! You are not here for nothing! God placed you here at this time in this season to fulfill Kingdom Purpose. You are special. There is only one you, and no one else can be you or do you like you can. Rise up and walk into your calling — you have been ordained and sanctified for a day such as today.

God has called you to fulfill His purpose!

It is time to wake up, shake off this religious façade, and start walking in God's greatness and making a difference.

You have been assigned to bring the people *life* so that they may escape *death*, but you must first escape death for yourself. Until you escape death, you are lost because you are outside of the original intent. The authority, dominion, and power are a part of the original intent. So, until you find your way back home, you are living life without the tools you were given to succeed, and you are out of your *Rightful Position*.

When Adam and Eve decided to disobey God and put their faith and trust into the contradiction of God's Word, they relinquished their rights to the opposition, and evil was permitted legal access into their hearts and minds. *Death* was the outcome, as God commanded.

As a result, we are all born *dead* without *life*. We enter a demonic system, and we are lost a very long way from the original intent. This is why every human being born is searching to fill a void — because they feel an emptiness inside that cannot be explained. We are searching for *Truth* and *Life* and just need to know the *Way*. We are out of position, something is off, and we feel lonely and incomplete because we are outside of the original intent.

You will never find what you are searching for outside of God the Father, Jesus the Christ, and the Holy Spirit.

- Everything you are searching for is within God.
- You come from God.
- You are nothing without God.

You are here because God placed you here to fulfill His Purpose here in Earth as it is in Heaven.

Once you find your way back home and receive *Life*, you become an *Ambassador of the Kingdom*.

- You represent <u>*Life*</u> amid Death.
- You are a <u>*Light*</u> amid Darkness.
- You represent <u>*Truth*</u> amid the Lies.

You are now seeking to save that which is lost, so you can bring them back home to the original intent.

Think about it — it is hard to do this from Heaven. God does not need you in Heaven. God needs you here on Earth, representing and reflecting Him for others to see that there is a better way and a better option available to them that will fill the void that they are feeling on the inside.

Most of what the World's System allows us to see and prepares for us to take in as truth is nothing more than a fairytale. They pretend to give us a choice, knowing that whatever we decide will always benefit them and not us.

Are you not tired and fed up with going in the same circles?

There are new promises, new hopes and dreams, and new vision boards, but you get the same old outcome every time.

Nothing changes for you until you change yourself. That begins with the way you *think*, then the way you *speak*, and ultimately the *actions* you choose to take in the process.

1. *Think*
2. *Speak*
3. *Act*

We were made in the image and likeness of God.

Does it not make sense to spend time getting to know who God is, so that we are able to get a better understanding of who we are?

Now, don't get me wrong — I'm not stating that we will ever know who God is and fully understand God. I'm simply stating that it is crucial that we go out of our way to build a *relationship* with our Creator, so we can better understand ourselves in the process.

We have tried (and I am sure some are currently trying) everything else, and it has not worked or been successful.

Why not try God and see what happens?

- Try *God* — not religion.
- Try *God* — not rules, regulations, and traditions of men.
- Try *God* — not man-made foolishness.

God sent Jesus to provide a way for us to come back home to where we originally were before the willful disobedience of Adam and Eve. We are all born lost in sin, and Jesus is the only way back to our original intent and *Rightful Position*. Without accepting Jesus, we remain lost, no matter what the situation or circumstances may be. Jesus is the one and only way back home.

- *Jesus is NOT a Religion.*
- Jesus never started or created a religion.
- Jesus is simply the *Way*, the *Truth*, and the *Life*!

What else do we really need other than Jesus?

<u>*We do not need religion if we have Jesus!*</u>

This is why so many religions will preach and teach everything about God but nothing about the one and only way to the God they are preaching and teaching. Jesus makes it all clear and eliminates the need for man and all the religion man has conjured up to remain in control of you and your family.

If you are familiar with your Bible and the life of Jesus, then you know that we are clearly going through the same purposeful attacks of religion today.

Respectfully, the largest denomination in the world still tells their sins to a man who is full of sin himself, prays to the mother of Jesus, who is not the way to God, and reads out of pamphlets instead of the Bible. The largest denomination is nothing more than the same people Jesus rebuked over and over for lack of understanding and lack of *relationship*.

Then we have the Protestants, who actually use the Bible; however, all their systems are based on the same teachings and inaccuracies as the largest denomination, with a tweak here and there. The message of *relationship* is still non-existent, and religion remains the goal to control.

<u>*RELIGION IS A DESTROYER!*</u>

Religion enslaves you to the doctrines and traditions of men and keeps you far away from building an intimate *relationship* with God for yourself.

The more they encourage you to do what they want you to do, the more you remain blind to the actual Truth that Jesus came to reveal. Jesus came to seek and save the lost and to give us *abundant life.* Jesus came to free us from the chains and shackles of man, which ultimately are the demonic and Satanic attacks from principalities orchestrated through man by the Devil himself to keep us blinded and distracted from the Truth.

The harvest is plenty, but the laborers are few, and this is exactly why. We have people who think they are laboring for God but unknowingly hinder God's plans due to the lack of knowledge, corrupt practices of religion, and man-made rules and regulations that attempt to keep God's children trapped in the wrong system.

<u>*Only the Truth will make you free, and Jesus is the only Truth!*</u>

No substitution will suffice. If you do not have Jesus, you are lost, out of the original intent, and not in your *Rightful Position*. You are attempting to live and obtain life without *Life*, and that will never work in your favor.

We cannot expect to have *Kingdom results* and live a *Kingdom lifestyle* if we are mentally obligated to the World's System. This is a huge contributing factor to the confusion in the church today. Many so-called followers of the Bible attempt to obtain the power of God while simultaneously promoting and marketing the way of the world, which completely contradicts the Word of God.

Remember, this is exactly what Adam and Eve did in the Garden. They attempted to obtain the power of God by disobeying God's Word and putting their faith and trust into the contradicting words of the serpent. As we all know, that did not work out too well for Adam and Eve then, so how is it that we expect it to be any different for us now?

They (even those who may know it) will never say this or speak on it, mainly because it threatens their man-made positions and takes their control away.

I do not care about any of that because I know who I am, I know what I have been called to do, and like any other *Messenger of Truth*, I am prepared for what comes with it. I pick up my cross, and I follow after Truth, and I sacrifice myself to enlighten and empower others so the *Message and the Gospel of the Kingdom* will be preached to all nations as a witness instructed by Jesus Himself.

There is only one message Jesus sanctioned, and it is the only message not taught in seminary or in most churches around the world today. It saddens me that we do not read our Bibles for ourselves. We need to let God bring revelation and confirmation to us directly by His Spirit.

We are more interested in religion and denominations, the traditions of men, and arguing back and forth about foolishness than we are *Simple Truth*.

The Truth, although rarely accepted by the majority, is always enough because it is the Truth that makes you free! *Your freedom is in the Truth!*

Everything about the lie promotes and encourages slavery to keep you bound, lonely, depressed, and empty. Nothing about the lie is Godly or beneficial and productive for you or your family. *Religion is a lie!*

1. Religion enslaves.
2. Religion keeps you blind.
3. Religion isolates you and makes you lonely and depressed.
4. Religion is not fulfilling and leaves you empty.
5. Religion is Not a *Relationship* with God.
6. Religion is not beneficial or productive for you or your family.
7. *Religion is a Lie!*

GOD IS LOVE — Where is the *Love* in religion?

Be honest with yourself, really search within, and ask yourself: is it even possible to obtain all the promises of religion that are marketed and advertised to you as your savior and your way out?

And if religion is so great, then why does the world still suck so badly?

Why do things seem as if they are continually and consistently getting worse every day?

Why is religion not working?

Because most man-made religion has no God in it, that's why!

Most religion promotes hate and the opposition of love, and that eliminates God from the equation entirely. You do not have to be a theologian to put this together for yourself. You don't need Scientology or stargazers to conclude that religion is not working. This is simple.

Look at your life, look at where you are, and ask yourself: is this the best that God has to offer you? Is it religion or a *relationship* that will make the biggest change for you?

RELIGION IS NOT RELATIONSHIP!

Religion is a facade that makes you feel as if it's building a *relationship* while simultaneously distracting you from one entirely.

The Devil is crafty and has no new tricks. The same thing he did in the Bible is the same thing he is doing today because he knows it works very well.

Why should the Devil change if he knows what he is doing to keep people blinded and distracted is working?

Sadly, the Devil knows more Bible than most so-called followers do, and that is why he can use the power of the Bible to keep them enslaved because most people

<u>*DO NOT READ THEIR BIBLE FOR THEMSELVES.*</u>

A *relationship* begins with you knowing who you are, what you are, and who you belong to. You cannot and will not build upon what you don't know. Knowledge is not power; only knowledge that is utilized brings power. Knowledge without utilization is just that: knowledge. It means nothing and there is no benefit if you do not put it to work for you and your family.

It is time for a shift and a true renewing of the mind that brings about the change you need to eliminate the void in your life.

Whatever that may be for you personally, building a *relationship* with God will be the greatest thing you ever decide to do. There is nothing greater than knowing your Creator.

God is the Potter, and we are the clay. The clay is nothing without the Potter.

<u>*You are nothing without God!*</u>

God created you in his image and likeness. God is a Spirit, and those who worship God must worship God in spirit and in truth.

If God is a Spirit, and you were made in God's image and likeness, then you too are a spirit inside of and/or living in a body. You are not what you see when you look in the mirror. You are exactly what you do not see. The real you is tucked away, waiting to break free from the TRAP mentality and mindset of the World's System, in which you do not belong.

This is why there is such a battle within you that you cannot really explain, and religion, science, psychology, counseling, and all the man-made efforts will not help.

The natural man can only provide a temporary solution that will never suffice because it does not address the real you. Natural remedies will never solve spiritual fulfillment — it is impossible.

Once you realize and accept that you are out of position, you can begin to search for your Truth, and you will only find it in one name: Jesus.

Why do you think the world tries so hard and puts so much energy into you not respecting or acknowledging the name of Jesus?

There is no other name that receives more disrespect and less appreciation than Jesus.

Why is that?

History and even science have proven both the Bible and Jesus to be true, yet we treat Jesus as a cancer or some evil that must be eradicated.

Why?

Think of all the religions and belief systems of man and ask yourself which one is more disrespected than all the others combined? The world does not have a problem with your religion or your beliefs until you mention the name of Jesus!

Why is that?

The world is okay with prayer as long as you are not praying in Jesus' name. You can pray to statues, animals, false gods, and even to Mary with no issues, but as soon as you mention Jesus, the world has a problem.

Meanwhile, they praise and worship Satan live on stage on daytime television right in front of you and your children, and no one has anything to say!

How far we have fallen! Forgive us God for we know not what we do!

How disrespectful and ungrateful we are to not even acknowledge the name of Jesus while permitting Devil worship in our homes by way of television and radio every day!

Movies, cartoons, sitcoms, award shows, news, radio, and commercials all advertise, market, and promote demonic and Satanic darkness every day, so much so that it has become the norm, and most have accepted it with no pushback.

However, if a person mentions Jesus or Truth, the world comes to a stop in an uproar to eliminate, deny, and destroy it.

The World's System has a way of doing whatever they can to keep you enslaved and bound. You would think after all these years of dishonesty and inaccuracy that we as people would begin to see the repetitious trends. The Devil has no new tricks, and the same hustle he had in the Garden is the same one he uses today.

American history is proven to be a facade and a fairy tale. The system has been lying to us since the day we were born and has conditioned us to be the dumbfounded slaves strapped to a wheel much like the one in a hamster's cage that goes absolutely nowhere.

My assignment and my mission is to get you off this wheel of lies and empower you by the Spirit of God to walk in your Truth which is in, by, and through Jesus.

There is no other way to God or to the Truth but by Jesus. We must get back to our *Rightful Position* and original intent. We must wake up to the Truth.

The longer we walk around blinded by lies, the harder life will be because we are out of position.

Read between the lines. Chapter after chapter, I am reiterating the exact same thing over and over again, with the hopes that you will allow yourself to just get it. I have been sent to empower you to allow the Spirit of God to open the spiritually blinded eyes to see and to spiritually tune the natural ears to hear Truth over the lie.

Back to the Garden is a mentality and mindset that encourages you to *Know Who You Are*, get back in your *Rightful Position*, *Escape the Pig Pen* and get back to your Father's House so that you will ultimately walk in authority, dominion, and power as originally intended from the very beginning.

Religion will never provide you with what you are truly searching for in life. You need a *relationship* with God to fulfill your God-given purpose *not* religion.

It is better to listen now than to find out later. Do your due diligence, prepare accordingly, and take heed to the Truth, lest you continue to fall deeper into the lie.

Let it marinate deeply within your core — *Religion is <u>NOT</u> Relationship!*

Notes:

Chapter 6: Unequally Yoked and <u>MAN</u>ipulated

To be *unequally yoked* is to be tied down and enslaved to an agenda outside of yourself, causing a feeling of imprisonment. Only Truth brings freedom, and outside of Truth we can never be truly free. The Devil uses the people closest to us to keep us blinded by ignorance and the agenda of the World's System. This is detrimental to our growth and development.

The woman is supposed to be the helpmeet and the one who is supportive and beneficial to the man as he comes into the person that God has called him to be; however, as you can clearly see throughout the Bible, it is the woman who is usually the most detrimental.

The World's System has poisoned the woman and reversed her role into attempting to be the man rather than being the support the man needs. This is where chaos and confusion resides. God is not the author of confusion, so we already know that if confusion is present (and it is), it's the enemy and opposition at play.

Everything God has created is perfection. It is good in its original intent and *Rightful Position*. Once perfection and good is tainted with the opposition, you will find chaos and confusion. When we go outside of God and the original intent and step outside of our *Rightful Position*, we allow ourselves to be <u>*MAN*ipulated</u> and poisoned by the agenda of the World's System.

A man needs and desires the companionship of a woman, but the woman does not necessarily need or desire the companionship of a man, especially if she is not fully understanding of the original intent. Remember the woman was made for the man, and the man was already here alone and without, so the need and desire of the man is met and fulfilled by the woman that God provided. However, if the woman does not know her rightful place, and it is not taught or encouraged, then she may be perfectly fine not fulfilling her role and just doing her own thing.

The man is the head, which means he is supposed to be the covering and the leader. This also means he is the teacher. The problem is the man has lost his manhood and biblical understanding of what it is to be a man, and he has lost the woman in the process.

Satan is extremely crafty, and he has purposely and consistently caused so much confusion between the simplicity of the man and woman relationship that now men want to be with other men and women want to be with other women.

Respectfully, we don't have to pretend we don't understand the simplicity of how a puzzle works or how things created fit or don't. There is a stick and there is a hole, and they fit perfectly. Two sticks sword fighting doesn't make common sense, and two holes slipping and sliding will never connect. Again, Satan is crafty.

While most think that this is a personal preference and it is not that big of a deal, they fail to realize it is a direct and blatant disrespect to the original intent and natural order that God put into place from the very beginning. I have no judgment or condemnation either way because that is not my position or calling; however, we must be wise enough to see the Devil's agenda at play.

Anything and everything Satan does is in opposition to what God originally said, and this started long before the Garden. Satan was cast out of Heaven because he wanted to elevate himself above his *Rightful Position* and original intent. This is the same weapon he has used on man from the very beginning. If he can get you out of your *Rightful Position*, he can empower you to deny and willfully disobey the commands and directions of God, and this is the whole point.

The Devil does not care about you or your well-being. He only wants to use you to prove God wrong and to destroy your relationship with God in the process.

The way Satan can convince the man he doesn't need the woman and convince the woman to be with another woman is ultimately the same way he has convinced them both that they do not need God. Each empowers the other simultaneously, and this is why there is so much chaos and confusion.

Outside of God, there is no love, joy, or peace, but we are all looking for these things daily. Satan causes the emptiness by eliminating the Source and then promotes himself as the one who can provide the solution to the problem he created in the first place. Think about it. This is the way that the World's System works. They make you sick, and then the people who made the disease are the same ones who give you the antidote and/or cure. So, they benefit twice, and you suffer twice, all under the disguise of them "helping" you get better.

The World's System is full of fake choices that they push on you as the so-called decision maker, but you are being duped from the start. When your eyes are open to see, it is so plain to receive this simple revelation.

The Devil provides you the opposite of whatever God said, and no matter how it looks, sounds, smells, tastes, or feels, it is always a lie to discourage you from knowing the Truth. Again, only the Truth will make you free. To keep you enslaved is the Devil's agenda.

The man must know his role and the woman must know her role from a Godly and Biblical standpoint to fulfill their purpose.

Outside of the Truth is only the lie and the father of lies, and his agenda is to keep you trapped in the wrong system. Too many people are attempting to fulfill the wrong purpose, and then they wonder why they are not satisfied and why it doesn't ever seem to work out for them.

God is the Potter, and we are the clay. Without the Potter, the clay is *nothing*!

God is the Creator of ALL, and we are the created, and the created will never outweigh the Creator. Satan is also the created, and he continues to try to outweigh and outdo the Creator and <u>*MAN*</u>*ipulates* you to help him do it. What a pointless and exhausting task that leads to nowhere in the end.

Bottom line: men with men and women with women cannot and will never reproduce a thing except chaos, confusion, and disease, which are ALL a part of the agenda of depopulation!

- Men with men cannot produce children = depopulation.
- Women with women cannot produce children = depopulation.
- Men with men is unnatural and causes diseases = depopulation.
- Women with women is unnatural and causes diseases = depopulation.
- Men with men who adopt children may encourage the same = depopulation.

- Women with women that adopt children may encourage the same = depopulation.
- Men and/or women who decide to support abortion = depopulation.

Depopulation is Satanic and Demonic at every level and degree!

God instructed us to be fruitful and multiply, to replenish the Earth and subdue it.

Respectfully, God did not say be fruity and decrease, to depopulate the Earth and abort and destroy it!

This is a purposeful attempt of the enemy and opposition to defy God and our original intent.

Satan does not want the man and woman to know the power that they possess, and he will do everything he can to make sure they remain blind and deaf and outside of their *Rightful Position*, which God has already ordained and sanctified.

Man and Woman have major issues in their relationship because there is no leadership or guidance in the home!

The man has forfeited his place and no longer enforces his role due to the pure lack of the knowledge of who God has ordained and sanctified him to be.

It is the man's responsibility to lead, protect, and cover his home in the way that it should go, and it is the woman's responsibility to help, assist, and encourage the man in the process.

Respectfully, most men are very, very, very soft and weak! This new world has put so much pressure and weight on men that it seems that they have just given up on both life and their relationships altogether.

It is a sad sight to see: men who have chosen to find themselves in other men and/or men who have relinquished all their responsibilities and role of the man to women and then wonder why life is so challenging for them and why they have a hard time finding any peace.

My heart and sympathy go out to the women who were in relationships with men who one day decided that they were not good enough and allowed other men to take their place. What a devastating blow to the woman's character, personality, and security because of a man who could not be a man for himself or for her!

A Woman is not a Man, and a Man is not a Woman!

We each have our own roles and responsibilities that must be acknowledged, appreciated, respected, and adhered to for relationships to work in our best interests. What God has set in motion, let no man attempt to change or override, as it will only bring chaos, confusion, and destruction to the home and the relationship.

God will not be mocked, and His Word will not return to Him void!

Satan has many men and women mocking God and His Word!

Men need to Man up and Women need to Woman up and be what God has assigned them to be. They must stop looking for alternatives and being <u>*MAN*ipulated</u> to be out of the original intent and outside of their *Rightful Position*.

Most people are *unequally yoked* within themselves even before they enter a relationship with someone else, and this is detrimental for all parties involved.

The most important factor in this equation is that a person must know who they are, who they belong to, and what they stand for, or they will fall for anything that is being shoved down their throat by the World's System.

Regardless of your choices, there is only one you in the whole world, and you are fearfully and wonderfully made.

You are one of a kind and you are special, and you were known by God before you entered your mother's womb.

Do not allow Satan and the World's System to dictate who you are and define you!

You must Know Who You Are for yourself!

To be equally yoked begins within and starts with knowing who you are and who you belong to and who it is that allowed you to be here in the first place.

- How will a relationship outside of yourself ever work if you don't even know yourself?
- How can anyone else fulfill you, or how can you attempt to fulfill anyone else, if you don't understand and know that you need to fulfill self-first?
- Relationships are challenging with God. How much more so will they be without God?

I want to be clear that I am writing this respectfully, with no judgment or condemnation, because I know many people who are on the opposite side of what I am disclosing here, some of whom I consider to be friends and care about deeply.

However, truth is always truth, and the truth is usually uncomfortable when it exposes the lie. Unfortunately, it usually hurts before it helps.

The way of this new world has promoted, advertised, and marketed so much darkness that it is difficult to see any bright lights anymore.

Even some of those who used to carry the light have been compromised and have chosen to join the darkness for their own selfishness and greed, at the expense of those they were placed here to protect.

There was a time when leaders would stand up against injustice and defend the rights of the people, but now they are proponents, pushing the very agenda that they were once against.

No longer can we look to the leaders of this tainted world and trust that they have our best interests in mind. And this goes for all so-called leaders, not just world and government leaders. Compromise is rampant amongst them all, including church and religious leaders.

Think about it:

- Who did Jesus have the most problems with in the Bible?
- Who were the ones who did not accept Him?
- Who were the ones who falsely accused Him and had Him crucified?

Truth is the only thing that makes us free, and Satan has convinced those who used to tell the truth that the lie is more beneficial and productive for them.

Let God be the Truth and every man a liar, and stop allowing yourself to be *Unequally Yoked and <u>MAN</u>ipulated* by the World's System. Get *Back to the Garden* in your *Rightful Position* where you belong.

Notes:

Notes:

Chapter 7: "Escape the Pig Pen"

The wages of sin is death, but the gift of God is eternal life in, by, and through Jesus. We don't need man or the traditions of men to be satisfied. We simply need Jesus. This is not difficult to grasp.

The Creator of All is the best of all. Nothing created will ever outweigh its Creator. All power is in the one and only name of Jesus. Jesus is the vine, and we are the branches. There are no branches without the vine, and there is no fruit without the branch.

Know Who You Are. Know your position, and find your purpose, so you are able to fulfill *Kingdom Purpose.*

Every day you wake up, you are on assignment, so you must know who, what, when, where, and why, and you must have the wisdom of how. You are only a benefit if you have knowledge that can be shared with others so that they do not perish outside of their original intent.

The lack of knowledge is what destroys people. The Devil takes full advantage of this to maximize on your ignorance for his demonic agenda. Satan wants to destroy you and your family and keep you blind and deaf to the Truth.

Truth will always be the World's System's enemy because Truth exposes lies and the father of lies.

Have you ever noticed how different the outcome is when the Truth gets involved or is added to the equation?

Lies, Lies, Lies... then one speck of Truth, and boom — *CHAOS!*

Truth brings life to eliminate death, and Truth seeks out the lost to bring them back home.

Satan does not want you anywhere near home because he knows this is where your authority, dominion, and power reside.

Satan will do everything he can to keep you away from your power, and he will use any means, including religion, to do it. His main goal is to keep you bottled up in the lies and as far away from Truth as possible, with the hopes that you will _live_ and _die_ within the lie.

Your goal must be to get out of the lie and the system of lies and back to the Truth. Your true freedom is in the Truth, and it is only the Truth that will make you free.

Real Freedom is only in the Truth. The Truth has a name, and it is _Jesus!_

- Why do you think this one name causes so much controversy?
- Why do you think the system of this world goes out of its way to eliminate this one name?

Think about it. The world does not have an issue with religion, denominations, cultural groups, gangs, mafias, or cartels. The world clearly supports and promotes these to you daily, but the name of Jesus is blasphemed, ridiculed, crossed out, and attacked from every angle. Why?

Even Bible-toting so-called believers of Christ won't honor and revere his name in prayer, to avoid "offending" anyone else. Meanwhile, they are disrespecting and dishonoring the one they are praying to, who likely never even hears the pointless, nameless prayer anyway.

Satan is crafty and has his hands in all aspects of religion, whether you know, see, or understand it or not. Satan's goal is to keep you distracted from the Truth. If that means providing alternative ways to God, getting you to pray to Mary or worship the sun, moon, stars, cows, and statues, or simply entertaining you every Saturday or Sunday in a church, mosque, and/or temple, then that is exactly what he does.

Again, think about it — it is okay to pray and say amen or mention Muhammed, Buddha, and many others, just as long as you don't mention the Truth.

Look at the man-made holidays that have been <u>*MAN*ipulated</u> to obtain a benefit from both ends of the spectrum. The world created Christmas and Easter but then gave us Santa Claus and a demonic bunny that lays eggs to distract you from the Truth of the day. Then they provide you with a "shortcut" that eliminates the Truth, and even the so-called believers use it: *X-mas*.

How disrespectful yet crafty is this Devil?

Even the so-called elect fall for the foolishness and lies!

My people are destroyed by the lack of knowledge. Stop allowing this demonic and Satanic system to dictate who you are. Stop taking everything provided to you as matter of fact without any due diligence.

If you want more out of life, you must simply do more to understand life. There is no life outside of Jesus, only death and more death. The walking dead are after you and your family to fulfill the agenda of Satan and to keep you enslaved in the lie.

You are either with God or against God. There is no middle ground or purgatory or any of this other foolishness they shove down our throats. You are either with Christ or Antichrist.

This is not difficult to understand; this is simple.

The God of the Bible is the Father of All and the one true God. There is only one way to Him, and that is in, by, and through Jesus.

- Jesus is the only *Way to* God.
- Jesus is the only *Truth of* God.
- Jesus is the only *Life from* God.

No one comes to God the Father unless it is in, by, and through Jesus.

<u>*You must have Jesus!*</u>

The world attacks the name of Jesus because it is the Truth that exposes the lie and the father of lies. You must cut the strings from the Satanic puppet master, and you must get off the hamster wheel that goes in a fast rotation to absolutely nowhere.

Do your due diligence and think for yourself. Seek to build a relationship with your Creator and know the Truth that will really make you free. Reject the facade of freedom that purposely keeps you trapped in the lie.

Satan is a liar!

He hates you and everything you stand for — even if it is him.

- You remind him of someone he envies.
- You remind him of someone he wants to be.
- You remind him of the "could of, should of, would of" that will never be.

The Devil has a simple goal to destroy you and your family and to try and prove to God that we are unworthy of and ignorant to the Truth. Sadly, he does a great job of keeping us in the *Pig Pen*, even after we have come to realize the Truth, and he uses religion to do it.

It is time to get out of the mud and go back to your Father's House!

I write this message to you with a heavy heart, knowing that most will be naive and ignorant to the Truth because of the brainwashing and conditioning of religion and the traditions of men. For far too long, we have sat back and trusted the so-called leaders of this world to point us into the right direction and to do what is best for us and our families.

Unbeknownst to us, their agenda is to do the exact opposite so they remain in a position of control over us.

They do not want you to obtain the Truth. If you find your own power, they will lose their power over you. You will begin to think for yourself and eventually unite with other like-minded individuals who all want what's best for themselves and their families.

Man and the traditions of men are not your answer — <u>man cannot save you!</u>

Get out of the *pig pen* mentality and mindset. There is a well-known saying, "Get it out the mud." I just need you to get you out the mud. I need you to experience the "a-ha moment" that changes you to be what God has ordained and sanctified you to be. Then you can take that knowledge and that purpose to seek and to save others who are lost, away from home, and still playing around in the same mud in the *pig pen*.

<u>Your whole purpose is to fulfill Kingdom Purpose! Nothing more and nothing less.</u>

So, what is this *pig pen* we must escape from?

Note: For those of you who have a Bible, I recommend that you read <u>*Luke 15*</u> in its entirety (preferably the King James Version) before reading further.

Jesus provides us with a wealth of knowledge pertaining to our lives and the importance of the transition from one system into the other by the renewal of our minds.

There are two systems at play here in the Earth realm. You have the World's System, which is the natural, and then you have the Kingdom of God, which is the spiritual. The spiritual always goes before the natural, so we are always playing catch up to what has already been spoken.

Back to the Garden is a mentality and a mindset that places us in our original intent and *Rightful Position*, with a clear understanding of who we are and the authority, dominion, and power that God has equipped us with from the very beginning.

Jesus speaks in a manner within Luke 15 that correlates with Adam and Eve in the Garden. To be lost, you must have been there and for there to be death there must have been life first.

The part of Luke 15 I want to focus on right now starts with Verse 11, but I definitely encourage you to read the whole chapter for clarification and confirmation.

Verse 11. And Jesus said, A certain man had two sons:

Verse 12. And the younger son said to his father, Father, give me the portion of goods that are mine. And the father divided unto the younger son his portion of the goods.

Verse 13. And not many days after the younger son gathered all his portion of goods, and took his journey into a far country, and there he wasted his portion of goods with riotous living.

Verse 14. And when he had spent all, there arose a mighty famine in that land; and he began to be in want [need and lack].

Verse 15. And he went and joined himself to a citizen of that country; and he sent him into his fields to feed swine [pigs].

Verse 16. And the [younger son was so hungry he longed to] have filled his belly with the husks that the swine [pigs] did eat: and no [person] gave unto him.

Verse 17. And when the [younger son] *came to himself*, he said, How many hired servants of my father's have bread enough and to spare, and I perish with hunger!

Verse 18. I will arise and go to my father, and will say unto him, Father, I have sinned against heaven, and before [you].

Verse 19. And am no more worthy to be called [your] son: make me as one of [your] hired servants.

Verse 20. And the [younger son] arose, and came to his father. But when he was a yet a great way off, his father saw him, and had compassion, and ran, and fell on his neck, and kissed him.

This is exactly where we are today — a great way off from the Truth — but God the Father has compassion on us and provides us with His best in, by, and through Jesus.

Just like Adam and Eve and this younger son, we want to go out and do our own thing rather than abide in the Truth. Adam and Eve were kicked out of the Garden we need to get back to, and the younger son was in the same *pig pen* we need to get out of.

The *pig pen* is the World's System in which we reside, and we so desperately need to *come to ourselves*, get back to our Father's House, and take our *Rightful Position* as joint heirs and children of the Kingdom. We are in this world but not of this world. The *pig pen* is the system of the world, but it is not our intended system. You must get yourself out of the mud and *Escape the Pig Pen* mentality and mindset.

You are supposed to be with your Father at your Father's House, which is the mentality and the mindset of the Kingdom of God. You do not belong in the *pig pen* with the *pigs*!

You must Escape the Pig Pen!

Many people who have confessed with their mouths and believed in their hearts that Jesus is Lord and that God has raised Jesus from the dead are saved to escape Hell but are still enslaved and trapped in the *pig pen*. They seek God and accept Jesus but have never heard or been empowered by the only message Jesus ever preached, and that is the Kingdom.

Pastors and preachers spend a lot of time preaching Jesus and what Jesus did but never speak on the things that Jesus spoke about.

The only message Jesus ever preached is the Kingdom of Heaven and the Kingdom of God!

So, how often are you hearing the only message Jesus ever preached from those who have the platforms to speak?

The Bible, both the Old Testament and the New Testament, is written about the King and His Kingdom. If you do not understand this, then you are still in the *pig pen* with the *pigs*.

Take this opportunity to *come to yourself* and *Escape the Pig Pen*.

I sincerely pray that you receive your "a-ha moment" and decide to go back to your Father's House where you belong and originally came from.

We were given a system that equipped us with the authority, dominion, and power to subdue the Earth, but we gave it all away when we decided to disobey the Word of God and place our faith in the word of the serpent.

This is the same thing the younger son did in the parable. He was at home in his Father's House with his Father, just like Adam and Eve were in the Garden with God.

In the Garden, Adam and Eve had access to and authority over everything, with one simple commandment of what not to do to jeopardize it all. The younger son is in his Father's House with his Father, and he has access to and authority over everything his Father possesses yet still wants to go out and be on his own, just like Adam and Eve wanted to be like gods.

When Adam and Eve disobeyed God's Word, they transitioned their authority to Satan and entered another system in which they did not belong. When the younger son decided to leave his Father's House, he too transitioned from his authority in his Father's House into a new system in which he did not belong.

As we can clearly see, being outside of our *Rightful Position* and the original intent never works in our favor because it is not our system. The World's System is a demonic and Satanic TRAP to keep you in death and away from the *Way*, the *Truth*, and the *Life!*

The first sign of Godlessness is *Fear*. The first thing Adam and Eve did in fear was look to the trees for leaves to cover their nakedness. The first thing the younger son did in fear was look to man for help. Neither of these options is sufficient. God does not give the spirit of fear. When you are in fear, you are out of position. Adam and Eve hid from God due to fear, and the younger son put his trust in man due to fear.

Hiding from God and trusting man will never help!

Disobeying God, hiding from God, wanting to be like gods, and fear got Adam and Eve put out of the Garden. Wanting to do his own thing, riotous living, putting his trust in man, and fear got the younger son into the *pig pen*.

Adam and Eve were as close to God as they could ever be before they violated God's instructions, and the younger son was in a better position with his Father in his Father's House before he decided to depart.

They all decided that what they had was not good enough and chose to transition from their *Rightful Position* and original intent into a system in which they did not belong.

This is exactly what we are doing today!

Some of us are hiding from God in disobedience, and others are putting their trust in man and remaining hungry for Truth.

Jesus is the Truth you are desperately seeking!

Too many saved followers of Christ are still playing in the mud with the *pigs* because they place their trust in man and depend on man and the World's System to provide what only their Father can and will provide for them. It is time to wake up and *Escape the Pig Pen* mentality and mindset that keeps you trapped by religion and the traditions of men.

I need you to see yourself in this parable, have your personal "a-ha moment," and come to yourself and choose to get back to your Father's House. Break away from all the man-made foolishness that keeps you in the mud with the *pigs*, and seek your Father's House.

Luke 15:

Verse 21. And the [younger son] said unto [his Father], Father, I have sinned against heaven, and in [your] sight [Father], and [I] am no more worthy to be called [your] son.

This is a sign of sincere repentance, a true confession of the knowledge and acceptance of the wrong, a desperate willingness to receive forgiveness, and the attempt to make it right, but also understanding that we are not worthy or righteous ourselves.

The Bible declares that there are none righteous, no, not one and that our goodness is as filthy rags. This is why it is not by your own might or power but by the Spirit of God that you are able to do all things.

Verse 22. But the father said to his servants, Bring forth the best robe, and put it on him; and put a ring on his hand, and shoes on his feet:

Verse 23. And bring [here] the fatted calf, and kill it; and let us eat, and be merry:

Verse 24. For this my son was dead, and is alive again; he was lost, and is found. And they begin to be merry.

Notice how simply this transition back to his Father's House takes place. He comes to himself, makes a choice to go back home, and simply confesses and repents. Verses 22-24 are the result.

So, why do religion and the traditions of men make something so simple so difficult?

Notice what the Father did not say: go and take a shower and be cleaned with water before I place the robe, ring, and shoes upon you. *No* — he accepted his son as he was when he came and *immediately* put him back in his *Rightful Position* and original intent.

Do religion or the traditions of men follow this biblical outline for salvation?

No, they do not, and this is why there are so many saved people who continue to dwell in the *pig pen*! It saddens me to my core.

You will not receive the treatment of your Father's House when you are out of position, playing in the mud.

You must *Escape the Pig Pen* and make your way back home to your Father's House.

Notice the Father states that his son is dead, just like God told Adam and Eve if they ate of the fruit of the tree of the knowledge of good and evil that they would surely die. Now, we know that Adam and Eve and the younger son were not physically dead and very much physically alive. However, they were spiritually dead and out of their *Rightful Position* and original intent.

The younger son is alive again only after *coming to himself* and the sincere repentance for forgiveness. Keep in mind, it is also possible to come to yourself, repent, receive salvation, and then remain in the same system in the *pig pen*.

This is my whole point in writing this chapter. One will never receive the authority, dominion, and power of their Father's House when they are outside of their *Rightful Position* in the *pig pen*. Many people are saved and alive but still very much so lost, attempting to live a Kingdom life trapped in a World's System mentality and mindset.

Satan is extremely crafty!

He uses the same Bible you tote around to condemn you and keep you trapped in the *pig pen* even after you have come to yourself.

This is why there are so many broken and hurting people who are constantly waiting on God and not understanding why this religion and church stuff does not ever seem to work for them.

God is the Truth, and every Man a Liar!

You cannot and should never put your trust in man. It was the way of man and the World's System that put the younger son in the *pig pen* in the first place, and it is no different today.

MAN IS NOT YOUR GOD!!!

The traditions of men keep you in the *pig pen* and far away from your *Rightful Position* at your Father's House. The younger son was lost, but then he was found. This is how you *Escape the Pig Pen*! You go from spiritual death to life and from being lost to being found. This is why Jesus came to seek and to save that which is lost. Jesus came to bring you *Back to the Garden* and give you the authority, dominion, and power that God equipped you with from the beginning.

This World's System is not our system. The *pig pen* is the World's System.

The *Kingdom of Heaven* and the *Kingdom of God* is our Father's House.

We must transition back to the system in which we belong.

God controls the Kingdom, and Satan controls the World's System. For you to live your best life, you must partake in the right system. There are only two real options.

So, choose you this day which system you want to be a part of and whom you will serve.

The Kingdom or the Pig Pen?

Please understand in obedience I write this to inform you of Truth, knowing that it's a sacrifice to deny myself, pick up my cross, and follow Jesus. Like Jesus, I will be ridiculed, mocked, threatened, and hated by many. God has chosen a few of you who will have eyes to see and ears to hear and be empowered to seek and save that which is lost.

I will not expound on verses 24-32 of Luke 15 here in this book, but I encourage you to read it and understand that the elder son is an example of the "holier than thou" and religious people who are stuck in the traditions of men — so much so that he was not even happy about his own younger brother coming back home.

The other important factor to acknowledge is that he was with his Father, in his Father's House, and was not in the *pig pen* but still lacked the understanding of his *Rightful Position* and had a *pig pen* mentality and mindset.

This is so much a reflection of the church and religion today.

How sad is it that most people still cannot get along with one another?

This does not please God!

We Must Escape the Pig Pen!

Notes:

Notes:

Appendix

It is extremely important that you invest your time and energy into finding out exactly what it is that has you bound, locked down, and depressed.

This is what has you outside of your *Rightful Position* and original intent. You must experience your own personal Exodus, but you must first know and understand what it is you need to be made free from.

This seems simple and easy enough, but it is usually one of the most difficult things for a person to do because it means admitting failure due to brainwashing and conditioning. You must be prepared to accept that you have been a victim of the hustle due to your own ignorance and emotional vulnerability.

Most people have a hard time being honest with themselves, but this behavior is not beneficial or productive to growth and development. We must escape the fairy tales and get back to the Truth.

The Lord is strong and mighty and has the power to deliver you from under the hands of anyone and anything that hinders you. The Lord is greater than all and above all, and there is nothing impossible or too hard for the Lord.

Make a decision to look to the hills where your help resides. Lean not unto your own understanding, and in all your ways, acknowledge the Lord. Greater is the Lord that is within you than the foolishness of the world.

Break away from the rules, regulations, religion, and the traditions of men, and seek ye first the *Kingdom of God* and *God's Righteousness*. Allow God to direct your path and lead you beside the still waters. You can do all things through Jesus Christ who strengthens you and provides you the *Way*, the *Truth*, and the *Life*. Not by your own power or your own might but by the Spirit of God, you will overcome the challenges of life that attempt to hold you away from God's Greatness.

You have a purpose to fulfill, and every day you wake up, you are on assignment for the King of Kings and the Lord of Lords to fulfill that purpose.

My prayer is that you will *Make It Personal*, fill in the blanks below for your life, and not stop reading this book and the Bible until you truly *Know Who You Are!*

Before I entered my mother's womb God knew me, ordained me, and sanctified me to be _____ among the nations.

And I said, Blessed be the LORD, who has delivered me out of the hand of the _____, and out of the hand of _____, who has delivered me from under the hand of _____.

Now I know that the LORD is greater than all _____: For in the thing wherein they dealt proudly the LORD is above them.

Bonus Chapter: reDefine Thought
{Podcast Hosted by Joshua B. Hayes}

Joshua: Everyone welcome to r*eDefine Thought*. I am ***Joshua Hayes***, and today, I have my brother here — you know, in my life, a prime example of someone that did a complete change from who he once was and who he is today, and his story is pretty amazing.

I know a lot of people that used to be in his situation, never made it out, and maybe with his words that he can say today can help a few young people — or even old — to rethink about the situation they are in and give them some motivation, inspiration to change their life like he has changed his.

So, without any further ado — thank you, brother. I'm going to allow him to introduce himself.

Brian: Well, firstly, I appreciate the introduction, man. r*eDefine Thought* is extremely pertinent, it's powerful, it's definitely something that takes us into a different mindset and a way of thinking. Even just the word in itself makes me think.

But anyhow, I am ***Brian Lucas***. I have been a real estate investor for about twenty years; self-employed business owner, entrepreneur for seventeen years; licensed real estate agent/Realtor for fourteen years; publisher/author for five years. I currently own and/or manage seven businesses: real estate investing, buying, selling, renovating, and many other aspects of real estate; business management, start-up, credit building, debt management, budget planning, marketing, publishing, recording company, and most recently, a cleaning company for about two years.

So, it's safe to say I have been fortunate enough to make it around a couple of blocks. We're actually in the process of building three more companies: a design and consulting company, we've got a bakery coming, and life coach/mentoring.

So, we've got a lot…and I'm not big on titles, but just so everybody kind of gets an idea of where I'm at right now in comparison to where I was… I had to r*eDefine Thought*.

So, that's pretty much who I am, Brian Lucas, entrepreneur, business owner, author, and amongst other things that God has allowed me to do in forty years' time.

Joshua: That's a lot of businesses. You seem very, very busy.

Brian: Very, sir.

Joshua: I don't know how you even have time to do this right now.

Brian: I make time for what's important, sir.

Joshua: Well, I appreciate that.

Brian: You're welcome.

Joshua: So, you have all these titles now… entrepreneur, businessman. What kind of titles did you have before all this came? What would they call you?

Brian: That's an excellent question, and I hope your listeners are ready for these answers. I would have been a gang member. I would have been a street (for lack of incrimination)… a street person. Something that you would see on TV that most people don't really know anything about it.

I would have been the "you won't make it to see 18, you won't make it to see 21, you're going to spend the rest of your life in prison."

I would have been the epitome of the definition that the world tries to define for a person of my status. And yeah, I think that's the best way for me to answer that. I would have been everything but what I just mentioned previously.

Joshua: And that's crazy. And we can throw one in there for people who can't relate to just that street stuff. You could say high school dropout. Right?

Brian: Naw...I would just say, never made it to high school dropout.

Joshua: Dang, never made it. Jeez.

Brian: Never made it to high school. I went to ninth grade three years in a row because I went on vacations during the first two years...all three years, actually. I had away from home vacations, and I actually ended up getting my GED at the age of seventeen years old with high rankings.

I know that sounds really ridiculous because most people don't really understand GED unless you had to be in that situation. But I mean, I was not an ignorant, or shall I say uneducated, child. I was very, very smart, but I was also very, very bored.

And that's why everybody is built differently, like the mentality, the mindset that we have. And another reason it's really important — and I hope I'm not going on a tangent, but I may be — that we have a goal in place, especially for children who are smart or may be a little bit ahead of their class or whatever the case may be.

Because those particular children, if they're not challenged in a way that's positive, they will find something negative to do. I'm a living example, and I'm talking from experience, not from something I read in a book. I was extremely smart as a child. I was in honors and accelerated classes, and what I found myself becoming was somebody who was extremely bored with the way that school was run.

So, I found myself getting into trouble because they could not challenge me mentally the way that I needed to be challenged at that particular time. And again, we're talking about years ago; this is way before there were all these tech schools. All this stuff that they have now wasn't around when I was in school.

So yeah, you have children who are smart but who may be getting in like little things of trouble now. Catch them now. Give them something to do to motivate them to set goals and to try to accomplish goals and try to keep them busy with things that are positive because it's really, really easy for negative things to creep in.

Joshua: Yeah, especially today. They have so much access to everything with social media and all this internet.

Brian: It is, and with you saying that, that's why people (especially people in their forties and fifties), you really need to understand that the dynamic is different. The dynamic is not the same because I was in my twenties before I had a cell phone. These children are seven and five with cell phones and know how to work them better than we do. Know how to work them better than we do.

So, the dynamic has changed, which means the opportunity to do the negative thing and the positive thing, but more so for most people who don't have those opportunities to get yourself in trouble.

There is access to the world, the worldwide web…www. That's what that means. The world wide web. When we were dealing with things in our circle, the farthest it got was school or church or whatever program you may have been in — boxing or karate, basketball and football. That was pretty much it. You had your bubble.

But now children are being challenged with things all over the world. And that means somebody that's in a completely different country can make your child feel bad about themselves, which is ridiculous. So, the access now opens up the door to a whole other realm of possibility to attack your home, your children, and the mindset and the mentality that we have, way more than it was for me when I was a child. So, I really... man, I have to keep children in prayer, like all the children, all around the world, cause what they're doing and what they're going through now, most parents don't even understand. They really don't understand because the dynamic has shifted so much, and it moves so fast.

Technology has moved so fast; you can barely keep up. Like there is a new phone every year with new technology. The phones... I guess Jordans... it's the only thing I can really think of that came out so much... that and CDs back in the day...see, that right there gives me away. They don't even have CD stores anymore. But Jordan comes out with a different shoe every year, and now the phone people are like, you know what, that's a good concept.

Every year, technology has shifted. I'm still the person — I get a phone when I need one. You know, I'm not really with the fads and everything else, but so many dynamics have changed that it just makes you have to position yourself to be a lot more knowledgeable, careful, and wise in pretty much all situations, or you will find yourself in a bad spot.

Joshua: Yeah, I think that's why it's important to have these podcasts and these conversations like this, when we are talking about _reDefining Thought_ because a lot of kids aren't growing up being taught to have a strong mind on things. So, if they don't have a strong mind or a strong stand or some type of morals or whatever, then they quickly can fall for anything that's going on in this world.

Brian: Absolutely true, and again, I went on a tangent — let me circle back. I was not a dumb kid. I mean, I don't know the word to use. I know everybody is so sensitive now. I didn't have problems and challenges in school. I wasn't a bad student. I was extremely smart. And that's not just me putting on — I know I was extremely smart because they test you for these things. I was extremely smart, and I found myself in a negative situation, going the opposite direction of where I should have been going without all the opportunities.

So, if me being smart was still a victim of negativity, gangs and street life, and all the different things that come with that, and that was then… now, there are so many more obstacles and challenges. And if the kid isn't smart, I mean, it's so easy to fall into negativity, and if you don't have, again, positives like this and many others, and just people who actually care about other people – not about what they can get from the people but actually care about people, and want them to do better, grow, develop, think for themselves, and not be swayed by the way of the World's System.

Not by thinking the way that the world has shoved down their children's throats and adult's throats the way you should think, because I see grown-ups my age that are acting like children, and that is not a judgment — that is the reality of it. There are grown-ups who have not really figured out who they are. And in the process of not figuring out who they are, they've had children, and they haven't been able to figure out who they are themselves. So, they can't direct and instruct and parent the child to figure out who they are either. So, now all of them are going in the same direction of the system that ultimately leads to a big, dirty, dry, lonely ditch.

Joshua: Well, I'm not big on reading; I'm big on listening to audio books. So, there's this audio book that I'm halfway through called *Outwitting the Devil* by Napoleon Hill, and it's basically talking about what you're talking about now. The word they used was "drifting."

People are drifting, and they don't have any focus. In their cycle of drifting, that's when the Devil is stepping in and manipulating their minds 'cause they're not thinking for themselves. So, he's adding a lot of fear, doubt, and worry. He's just attacking you while you're stagnant, basically. So, when you don't have any challenges in school, I imagine you're going to drift. And if you grow into an adult drifting, and then you have kids, you're just going to teach them to do the same thing that you're doing, which is drifting.

Brian: That's exactly right. You train a child in the way they should go, and they will not depart — and that goes for both the positive and the negative. Children are like cushions; they absorb everything. They are like sponges. They absorb what they are given. Again, I don't want to make excuses. I hate excuses, but we have to be realistic about it. We are a product of our environment — we don't have to be, but we are.

So, if you are setting this example in your household, in your school, or in your community; whatever they are accustomed to, that's what they're going to absorb. They're absorbing it and that's the direction they are going to go.

So, for me — and again, not making excuses because I don't like them — I didn't grow up in a household that didn't teach morals and ethics and responsibility. All that stuff was there. But at the same time, because I was ahead of my age group, I found myself hanging around people that were ahead of my age group. And what they were doing seemed way more interesting than what I was being taught.

So, I found myself as a thirteen-year-old really hanging around nineteen, twenty-year-olds, twenty-two-year olds, almost thirty-year-olds, and people my age now. In reality, at thirteen and fourteen years old, that did help me in a street perspective, and I would call that a positive because there are rules and regulations for the streets. There is a code. I mean, people don't really follow the code any more today, but I still live by it. There is a code, and that particular code really had to be taught. It's not something you just figure out. So, in all reality, even though it may have been a negative, it probably was some things that outside of God, of course, that He could have utilized to keep me out of harm's way. There is plenty of times I could have been killed or in prison for the rest of my life, had I not had someone with wisdom and knowledge from the elders in the streets.

So, the same concept needs to be utilized on the positive note. And it's not an excuse nor is it a crutch. Because I made a choice, but I didn't have many choices that were elevating me the way I wanted to be elevated. And again, taking myself into account, being selfish, a little greedy and a little – well, a lot naïve, really. Not really understanding what I was getting myself into, but seeing the opportunity within it, for lack of a better way of saying it.

So, the same opportunities that are there in the negative really need to be there in the positive, especially when you are younger. See, older people think in their mind that somebody's too young for something, but man, if it started with me at thirteen, in this day and age, it's probably more like ten or younger now. Like, we have to reach them when the opportunities are presenting themselves. At thirteen years old everything shifted in my life. And it's not because I became a teen; it's because I started thinking for myself. I started _reDefining_ my thought, utilizing the concept here, but I wasn't _reDefining_ it for the good.

I was _reDefining_ it for evil, bad, for negativity. For a life that wasn't the life that God had planned for me. It was a life that I'd seen that I liked and because it seemed interesting, and it was better than what I was doing, I geared myself and went in that direction. I pressed forward towards the negative prize.

Joshua: So, going into the character that you said you had while you were doing that street life, what moment had you wake up and turn that switch on and change?

Brian: Man, I'll never forget it. That's an excellent question, too, by the way. The moment my perspective on life changed. Man, seriously, I'll never forget it. I'm a visual person, so I like to try my best to paint pictures, but for a lack of time, I won't go in depth. I'll give you a basic breakdown, and this is why I'll never forget it. First of all, I know where I was, I know what I was doing, I know everything based off this concept I'm giving you right now. So, if you can picture it, again, I told you I was on several away from home vacations. We'll call it that. So, in this particular case I was away from home on one of my many vacations, and I received a letter from mom. And in that letter, it gave me probably the best truth and advice. And it was very simple. I mean, so simple, so simple. She basically told me word for word… And visualize this, before I say what she said or before I tell you what the letter said…In my mind, I'm full grown, fifteen years old. So, at this time, I'm fifteen. I'm a full grown fifteen-year-old, not the normal fifteen-year-old. I'm a full grown in my mind, not the normal fifteen-year-old. I'm an active gang member. I'm living an active gang member street life, and I think I have life figured out. You know, I think I got it going on. I got the girls. I got a little bit of credit in the streets, like I have a reputation. I ain't to be fooled with. You know what I mean. They know who I am. My name rings. They knew not to play around. I had a reputation, and this is not something I'm saying to showboat.

I just want to give you a picture of the way I'm thinking as a fifteen-year-old. I'm untouchable. I'm in a gang. I'm in the street life. I got the women. I got a little money. I think I'm doing it big. I'm doing what I set out to do, so in my mind I've got this thing figured out. Not to mention, you know, I'm in this vacation location, which, that alone tells you, you ain't got this figured out. If you had it figured out, you wouldn't be here.

So, I'm reading this letter, and I'm reading her words. And it was probably the hardest hit and the strongest kick of reality at that time in my life. Now, remember I'm saying I'm fifteen. I'm in my forties now, so of course it's been many other things since then, but at this particular time, at fifteen years old, it was the hardest punch to the face or kick to the head of reality that I had. And this is what it said. This is what the letter said. It was a full letter, but this is what my "a-ha moment" was, for me. What made me look at things differently. And she basically told me, "You need to **_Learn How to Play the Game_**." Word for word.

"Brian, **_you need to Learn How to Play the Game_**."

So, again, I'm fifteen; I think I got it all together. I'm doing what I have to do. I think I know it all. I think I have an understanding… I mean, I'm fifteen, which is retarded to say this, but it's just the truth. I'm fifteen years old, and that may not have been the best word. Again, people are so sensitive. I'm fifteen years old, and I have this thought process as if I have it together.

Meanwhile, I'm sitting on an away from home vacation. That's where I'm currently at right now, reading. I'm in this small room, by myself with no windows, on this vacation, and I'm reading this letter with no light, in the dark. I'm all alone, but I think I have it together. But nonetheless, "**_You need to Learn How to Play the Game_**."

It threw off a light switch inside of me that I can't even really explain. I can't really put words on it, but it was an "a-ha moment" for me. It was much needed. It was life altering; it was life changing. Now, when I say this, I'm fifteen, but this is when I started to think differently.

Now, did I change all my ways? No, I did not. Did I ever go on vacation again? Yes, I went on many more. But the thought process, as far as trying to figure out something outside of myself that I never really thought about, was the "a-ha moment" for me.

That letter that she wrote to me, and it was a full-length letter, might have been five or six pages, but the tone of that letter, what she was stating to me – which, this is word-for-word now — but throughout the whole thing, she was giving me explanations of how life is a game, and she was explaining it to me in a way at a fifteen-year-old age, even being as smart as I was, I could grasp the concept in the position that I was currently in.

And in that conversation, that letter — "**_You need to Learn How to Play the Game_**" — she explained to me very thoroughly, if I did not **_Learn How to Play the Game_**, that I would always be on away from home vacations and possibly away from Earth vacations, if I did not start learning how to play the game. Because the game is serious. The game is serious.

Now, here I am, I think I got this. I got the girls, I got a little money, I got a little street cred, I got a little reputation, but I didn't understand life. I thought I had game, but I had no game at all. Because I didn't understand that the life I was living, the life I was currently living at a fifteen-year-old age, away from home at the moment, I was losing that game. And I was falling into the exact dimension, mindset, and mentality that the system had already had in place for me before I was born.

And that was an eyeopener for me — so much so that I've used the very same thing in many conversations, in many conversations. In many mentoring sessions dealing with all types of business. Just something that helps somebody understand, you have to r*eDefine* your way of thinking. Your way of… it's just a powerful name. r*eDefine Thought* is just the perfect name for what you're doing here. You have to rethink everything. Most of what you have been told is not true. Most of it is fictitious. Most of it is fake. Most of it is phony.

The world itself has a system in place to keep you where you're at. And keeping you where you're at keeps the rotation going the way they planned for it to go. And again, I'm not an excuse maker. I don't want to give people crutches. I don't want to give people reasons to make excuses for where they are at. That's not my point, but at the same time, when you don't realize that you're in this wheel that goes in a circle, you're going absolutely nowhere until you figure out that you're on this wheel of a circle that goes absolutely nowhere. When you don't know it, then you continue to run like the hamster on this wheel, which is the way that the system has placed it for you.

So, this wording – again, I didn't completely shift at this time. But my way of thinking shifted at this time. Now, I utilized this, probably most people would consider still in a negative way, but it did shift me and change me to a way where I started looking at the system and life and the things involved in the system and life (which is one and the same) differently.

And that's what helped me see things in a different way, understand things in a different way, by getting out of my own way and stop shooting myself in my own foot. Stop making excuses. Stop blame shifting. Stop having all these different reasons why all these different things are happening to me rather than really understanding life is a game, and you better learn how to play it.

Joshua: My takeaway from what you just said is that, you know, life is a game; you've got to know how to play it. But you are definitely going to lose if you don't take accountability for your actions, and you can't post blame on others for where you end up because at the end of the day the system might be in place, but you still have choices to make.

And your choices are fitting into the system. And that's why you're failing. And then, like you said, it's like a circle. If you don't take accountability for that then you are going to keep going in that circle like a hamster on that wheel. So, you have got to realize that you are in your own way. You are your problem; it's the choices that you're making.

Brian: Without a doubt. I mean, this is not a plug, but you know I wrote a book, *The Real Secret Behind the Secret of True Success*. And in that book — and it's not something that I'm the only one that's said this, because it just rings true — you are your worst enemy, and you also are your best friend. It's you that determines the outcome at the end of the day. So, we have to start looking in the mirror. Like, we can't keep using everything around us (which is a distraction, by the way) as the reason that we don't decide or make a choice to do such and such. Because at the end of the day, people do what they want to do, regardless of what you try to tell me and what you try to tell yourself. What's important to you, you do it.

Again, we just talked about…I won't even say what time it is right now. You know how busy I am. But I made it a point to be on here because I want to support the cause that you are doing because it's important. So, what's important to people, they make time for.

So, excuses and all these different things that we conjure up are crutches in life. We've got to stop it. We can't keep blaming… oh gosh, I want to go in a direction, but I won't because I don't want it to be offensive in any way. We really — and I mean people in general, no specifics — we really need to look at life for what it really is. We need to look in the mirror, and we need to start dissecting what the challenges and the problems really are. And we need to address those issues within. So, we can be a better person without. It starts on the inside of man, and when I say man, I mean man and woman. It starts on the inside of a person, because what's in a person is what's going to come out of the person. As a person thinks, so is that person.

Napoleon Hill, you just mentioned. He also has a book called *Think and Grow Rich*, which comes from "As a man thinketh within their heart so is that man," which is a Bible verse. And it's true, because what's inside of a person is what's going to come out of a person. Out of the abundance of the heart, the mouth speaks. So, what's in you is what's going to come out of you.

So, everything that we deal with, we have to start internally. Stop trying to blame the mirror; it's not the mirror. It's the person looking in the mirror. It's not the circumstances and situations around you; it's what the person in the mirror decides to make a choice to do in those situations that's around them.

Again, we are a product of our environment, but we don't have to be. But if we don't know that we need to learn to play the game, if you don't know that there is a game, if you don't understand that you are on a rotating wheel, you will continue to be on the rotating wheel. Once you figure out that there is a rotating wheel, and you're absolutely on it, then you have to make adjustments in your thinking. You have to r*eDefine Thought* so you can get off the wheel. I hope somebody gets that.

Josh: Well, you know, sometimes people just can't get it on their own. What do you suggest?

Brian: Well, I think circumstances…we're talking about different age groups here, too, so that's a very vague question. I don't know if I can really answer you directly. I will say first and foremost, no matter what age group you are…and when people hear that question, they probably immediately start thinking about stuff…and I know that's not what you meant. So, I want to make that really clear for anybody who heard that question. I know that's not what you mean. Most people would here that and go, "Yeah, how do I get this?"

No, what we are talking about here is how can we get into a position where we are able to see life for what it is and elevate ourselves even though there are challenges and circumstances. And my answer to that would be, first and foremost, you need to *Know Who You Are*. Point blank, simple, simple, no beating around the bush, no fluff, no tickling of the ears. ***You need to Know Who You Are!***

Now I can already hear it inside of you right now: "I know who I am." No, you don't. Most people have no clue who they are. And that is the first and foremost, the issue and the challenge that is in the mirror. ***You need to Know Who You Are.***

And that is so much deeper than we can ever finish in one broadcast. But you need to *Know Who You Are*. And I would almost beg the people who are listening to this to continue listening to *reDefining Thought*. Because what you're going to find… and I know you, I know your mindset. You already gave me the breakdown of what your goal is here. And that's why I'm so invested in helping and assisting in any way I can whenever I can because you are putting people in a position to think for themselves and to stop following the systematic approach that has already been laid out for them before they were born.

And most people don't even understand the wheel was already built for you before you got here. That wheel is a purposeful wheel, and it starts from the very first thing you do as a child outside of your home, which is go to preschool. It starts at preschool. And then it starts in kindergarten, and then it works its way all through the different layers of schooling.

And then you go to college. All these things are mechanisms… Now, I am not knocking education at all, but I am knocking the brainwashing elements of it, because it's not about educating you, it's about brainwashing you and putting you in a position that you will not be a threat later.

They are basically… that's the best word I can use, brainwashing you to be what they have already drafted for you to be. This is the concept that they have so you are already familiar with being somebody's employee, taking orders, going and doing this at this particular time, going to sleep at this time, eating at this time.

I mean, there is not much difference in the wheel than the vacations I just got through talking about. The only difference is you have a mindset that you think you're free. But even when you are free — because you don't have shackles on your hands, and whips and chains on your throat, and the things on your feet — because you are not bound, you still think that's freedom. That's not freedom. Slavery comes in all different types and aspects, and what we have governed ourselves to do in the wonderful United States of America is fall into this purposeful slavery — that we don't even know that's what it is, because in our mind, we have a choice. In our mind, we have a decision.

But you don't understand that the choices and the decisions that they are giving you both lead down the same road. Pepsi and Coca Cola, that's the same people. Verizon and AT&T, that's the same people. Republican and Democrat, that's the same people. Oh my gosh, I'm going on a tangent. But people need to understand… And I mean that in a way that you can understand it. I'm not saying you go look it up and say, "Oh, he's wrong. Coke and Pepsi, that's not the same people." Listen to what I'm telling you. They give you a choice, but you really don't have a choice. Because whatever you choose, the same people are getting the benefit, and it's not you. That's what I'm trying to say, so you need to *Know Who You Are*.

First and foremost, you must *Know Who You Are*.

When you look in the mirror, do you see who you are, or do you see who the world has told you that you are?

Do you see you, or do you see what the World's System has created you to be?

Do you think for yourself, or do you follow the next new thing that comes out?

This is the difference. You have been placed here for a purpose, and that purpose is to do what you have been ordained to do, what you have been sanctified to do, and what you have been born to do. You're not here for nothing.

So, when you look in the mirror, you need to *Know Who You Are* so you can figure out your purpose, so you can fulfill that purpose, which will help other people be elevated and grow and develop in the process.

So, if you're on this wheel…And I'ma help you out here…If you don't think you're on the wheel, and if you don't know about the wheel, and you don't even think there is a wheel… ooh, you're the best person to be on it, because you're already on it. And the fact that you don't believe there is a wheel that you are on means that you'll never get off it.

So, you are the perfect person for the system of the world because you are already indoctrinated and already conditioned. That's the word I was looking for. I kept saying brainwashed, and it is brainwashing, but conditioned is a nicer word. So, if you don't… because, you know, when you say somebody is brainwashed, they get defensive. "I'm not brainwashed!" Little do you know, you are brainwashed. But let's use the other word, which is conditioned.

They are conditioning you to be able to take orders. Why do you think you can have 5,000 people in a prison and only have 200 police officers? Think about that now. How do you think you can have a city of 20,000, but you only have a thousand cops? Because you have been conditioned already to fall in line. Because you are already on the rotating wheel that has started from the time that you are born. You have been indoctrinated with the system that basically gives you boundaries. And then in the process of giving you these boundaries, they tell you that you're free.

People need to understand that no matter what you're doing, at the top of this chain, at the top of this wheel, at the top of those strings that are attached to you, the puppeteers, they are the ones getting, and they are benefiting from every avenue you take.

So, if you want to talk about health, if you want to talk about food, if you want to talk about the pharmaceutical industry, if you want to talk about banking, if you want to talk about insurance, if you want to talk about all these different mechanisms that have been put in place… most of them mandatory now, by the way, if you think about it. It didn't used to be that way, but now they are. They all have the same hands in the same pot, and it goes from one to the next, and it goes in the same circle. It goes on the same wheel that most people are already on.

The enemy attacks you in the least thought-about area. You divide and you conquer. The enemy attacks in the places you don't think about. And let's be real, what's the two things that people are most vulnerable about?

You start talking about money… aww man, people get so quiet and get ghost. And you talk about food, man, they don't want to hear that. So those are the two areas that are prone to attack because they are vulnerable areas that people don't want to deal with which is why most people are broke and unhealthy.

Joshua: Well, to me, I think that going to the gym, working out, getting healthy helps you mentally as well as physically. So, you got to eat right, you gotta work out your body because it all comes together. So, if you're lacking in one, then the other is going to lack. So, if you're lacking in taking care of your body, your mind is going to lack. If you lack in taking care of your mind, your body is going to lack.

Brian: Because they are one and the same.

Joshua: Exactly.

Brian: I mean, we try to separate them, but at the end of the day, again, this all goes back to knowing who you are. When you *Know Who You Are*, these different elements are the governing factor of how you can exist on the planet. They are all one and the same. They are separate, but they are one and the same. So, I absolutely agree, if one area is lacking, something else is going to suffer.

Joshua: Yup, like your body's suffering, then your soul is suffering, you're unhappy, your mind's suffering, 'cause you don't see any good in yourself. And then, turn around — your mind's suffering, you're exhausted. You're negative all the time.

That's going to hurt your soul 'cause now your soul is negative all the time. And, you know, a negative person isn't going to be out there working out or eating healthy. They're going to be eating ice cream and some cake. They're going to get fat. They won't get out of bed 'cause they're depressed. So yeah.

Brian: And birds of a feather flock together. So, if I'm on this wheel — and we'll switch the wheel up to having a name now — if I'm on this negative wheel, all of it is the same thing — so people can get it. If I'm on this negative wheel, and I'm running on this negative wheel, if I see any company, it's because they are also on the negative wheel.

Birds of a feather really do flock together, and misery loves company. So, if one person is down and out, and the only people you have around you are down and out, you might want to rethink your circle because it's going to be really difficult to get on a positive note or get off that negative wheel if everybody on the wheel is running on the wheel with you and nobody is telling you how to get off it.

Right now… what you got right now is <u>reDefining Thought</u>. We're trying to elevate you to think… first of all, we want you to know there is a wheel. We want you to know that there is a conditioning, brainwashing wheel that practically everybody is on, and it's all at the same time. And we're doing all these different hypotheticals and giving you all these different criteria so you can think for yourself.

And we're doing it in a way that keeps us protected, too, because I could just flat out right tell you bluntly and directly what's what, but then we wouldn't have a show. There would be no podcast. There would be no show, so you have to get to a place where you start really looking at life for what life really is.

And going back to what my mom told me at fifteen, "***You need to Learn How to Play the Game.***" But in order to play the game, you have to know that there is a game. In order to get off the wheel, you have to know that there is a wheel. The longer that you act like you're not on the wheel, the longer you will continue to be on the wheel. The longer you act like brainwashing is not something that can happen to you, you will continue to be brainwashed. When you act like you can't be conditioned into thinking a certain way because that is the way that they want you to think, you will continue to think that way. Even the rejection of thinking that you're conditioned is also something that they have conditioned you to think.

Like when you hear the word "conspiracy theory." The conspiracy theory in itself is a conspiracy. The word in itself is something to get you off-centered of what's really happening. And it works all the time. Something is realistic and true, but because the world told you that it can't be true, they label it, "That's a conspiracy theory." And immediately your mind goes to, "Ahh, it must not be true." That's conditioning, that's what that is. You can't tell me it's not.

When you hear a conspiracy theory, those who are not adept to what it really is and what's going on, automatically go to, "Well, then, it must not be true," "Oh, it must be fake," "Oh, that's made up," when in all reality, that conditioning is the reason you completely disregard something when you hear "conspiracy theory."

Which is also how people get completely disregarded. Which, I won't go into that, but there's many figures that… entertainers and the like that you can think about that they completely write them off because they start telling you the truth. And because you're conditioned, you listen to the news and listen to all these different aspects of life that have already been placed there like seeds.

You... we... they gravitate towards being obedient to what we are hearing from the people that we hold at a high regard or think are in a position of leadership. That right there in itself is also a form of slavery. That's what that is.

Again, I try to be selective with my words, but some things you just can't get around. If you start thinking about this system in the way it really is, you will begin to start to see that a lot of you is not you.

And now, I didn't realize this at fifteen, not what I'm talking about now. But as I got older and started going through the system where I had to **_Learn How to Play the Game_**, I had to take the initiative and start to figure out this system that really isn't built to build us and develop us and to bring us into a place of prosperity and good success and health and wealth.

The system is not built for you to be a business owner. The system is not for you to run your own business. The system is not built for you to be in a position of power and authority and dominion, which has already been given to you from before you were born. The system is placed here for you to get in line — for you to help somebody else be a business owner, so you can help somebody else be a boss, so you can help somebody else prosper and have good success. That's the system that we're in.

So, once we figure out that the wheel exists, and we start to try to know who we are, then we need to figure out who we belong to. We need to know who we are, you need to know who you belong to, and you need to know what you stand for. And I'll leave it at that for this particular podcast. Just use your imagination. You need to _Know Who You Are_, you need to know who you belong to, and you need to know what you stand for.

Because then you can have a system within yourself — not from the system and from the wheel with the hamster running in circles. Something that you have already put in place for yourself. When you *Know Who You Are*, and you know who you belong to, and you know what you stand for, you begin to build your own systems. You begin to build your own definitions. You begin to become who you really are. You begin to look in the mirror, and you start to see yourself, not what the World's System has told you that you are.

You look in the mirror, and you start to see your own thoughts, your own ideas, and your own imaginations rather than what's been conditioned upon you — rather than what's been shoved down your throat since you were a child, rather than what the world wants you to see, wants you to think, and wants you to feel.

You start thinking for yourself. You start feeling for yourself. You start seeing people for who they really are, rather than what the system told you they are. You start having emotional attachments to things that you think are important, rather than what they told you is important.

And this is really, really important for you to grasp what I'm saying because so many people are so affectionate about how they feel and what they think, but they don't even understand when they look in that mirror, it's not even their feelings and their affections. It is the feelings of the conditioning that's been put upon them. It's not even themselves, and that in itself really should make somebody think because we all think we have it under control.

Like, when I was fifteen, and I'm on vacation, and I'm in a dark room by myself with no windows, and I think I got it together. Until I read this letter that tells me, you, Brian, need to **<u>Learn How to Play the Game</u>**. It was a punch in the face, man. It was a kick to the head because I thought I had it. I thought I got the game. I got the girl, I got the money, I got a little reputation. I got game. That's not what she meant, and I knew when I read it.

<u>You need to Learn How to Play the game.</u>

Joshua: So, not only does Mom's hands and feet hurt, her words hurt, too.

Brian: Absolutely. Again, we grew up in a household that had morals and ethics. We had what was right and what was wrong. We can't blame it on the way... all that stuff they can't do now, Yeah, we got it back then.

Joshua: It seems like her physical and her words did what it was supposed to do. It straightened you out.

Brian: Absolutely, again, train a child in the way they should go, and it will not depart from them. That's Bible, it's true. Whether you believe in the Bible, you believe in God or not, it's still rings true. The Word is true regardless. You train a child in the way they should go, it will not depart. I don't care what it is. It can be good or bad. Whatever you instill in that child, it will process, and it will show its face one way or another when they are of age. It's going to happen.

So, that's why you must be careful about what you instill in your children and the young people that are around you, in your communities, in your churches, in your schools, in your programs.

This is extremely important because if you pay attention to what's going on right now, it's the children that are under attack. They are going after your youth. The people that's going to be telling us what to do in the next fifteen to twenty years, that's where they are starting because they are smart. The World's System is not stupid. It may not be positive for the most part, but it's far from stupid. It's extremely wise. They are full of wisdom. They know what they are doing.

They're conditioning and brainwashing your children right now to do what the agenda wants to be done fifteen to twenty years from now. And I'll leave that at that because I'll go on another tangent and start talking about something completely different that we probably don't need to be talking about.

Joshua: That would be another podcast. You definitely got to talk about protecting our children 'cause they are being attacked, so…

Brian: Absolutely.

Joshua: Man, well, learned a lot, and it's definitely true that you got to *Know Who You Are*, and that's going to take some real constructive honesty. You gotta actually look in the mirror and realize who you really are and who you're being at this moment. It's not who you are. I know I had to, in my experience, separate it from everything that I was giving myself to, to finally see who I was. Who I was not who I wanted to be. I knew I could be better. I knew I was once better. So, you got to do that so you can start making some changes. But yes, yes… Thank you, sir, for your time, and tell everybody about your book again. Go ahead and plug it in one more time.

Brian: *The Real Secret Behind the Secret of True Success*, written in 2018. It is a very blunt, very direct, no holds barred truth. And it's not for everybody. It could be a little offensive because it's my attitude, direct and blunt with no fluff and no editing. It's pretty blunt, but in essence it's talking about the same thing.

You have to stop letting the world dictate the way you think and the way you act and the way you define yourself amongst the masses. You have to be in a position where you can take responsibility for your own actions, set personal goals to achieve, and stop making the excuses that are used as crutches to justify ignorance. And that can mean so many different things. And I know that we are wrapping it up, so I won't go into it.

But we have to stop making excuses and using those excuses as crutches to justify ignorant behavior or lack of knowledge. It's the lack of knowledge that destroys people, and we must stop blame shifting all our issues on everybody else and start looking in this mirror that I just got through talking about.

Stop allowing the World's System and society and the newest fad to define you. We have to r*eDefine Thought*. That's the subject matter of this whole podcast, this show, to r*eDefine Thought.*

And we have to learn to live by our own definitions that truly define us. So, when we look in the mirror, we start to begin to see who we really are and not all these different conditionings and brainwashings and thoughts and ideas and concepts that have been indoctrinated in us from the world.

And I can take it a step further, because I don't want people to think that I'm biased. From church, too, because these churches indoctrinate us with things that make us out to be somebody we're not.

Now, I'm not talking about The Church, I'm talking about churches, the buildings and all these different denominations and all this different stuff we have going on — that's a whole other show in itself. But all the indoctrinations from schools, from churches, from the system of the world, from society, from the new fashion, from what we should say, what we shouldn't say, what we should wear, what we shouldn't wear, how you should put your hair, how you shouldn't put your hair, what color should you wear, what you shouldn't wear... All these things are a distraction to divide and to conquer.

So, they conjure up all these different ideas and concepts that have everybody at odds with one another. While at the same time simultaneously making it seem like they are on your side to bring unity. It's wisdom in its strongest form, but it's not being utilized for something positive. It's being utilized as a detriment to the people. And when I say people, all people, because all people matter. So, all people, you're being hustled, you're being conned. You're being conditioned; you're being brainwashed not to be who you truly are and not to think for yourself.

And again, the words that I'm saying right now is strong... you just mentioned, her words, Mom's, were as strong as being kicked. I would say stronger because the hits and the kicks go away, but the words last forever.

Joshua: I don't know, I'm still feeling that pain from when I was eleven. Yeah, I think that's why my back is still hurting. But no, I totally agree.

Brian: I really appreciate you allowing me to contribute, to invest in what you're trying to do. I strongly believe it's necessary. And for those who are listening, I would just say, just keep listening… Life has so many challenges and so many struggles and so many consequences that we really need to be in a position that we start taking on this responsibility to develop ourselves, our mindset, our mentality.

Start thinking for ourselves. Think outside the box, think inside the box. Just think, think for yourself. It can be in the box, outside the box; you can be laying on the box. It doesn't matter, just start thinking your thoughts, not the thoughts that are being indoctrinated into you. Start thinking your way rather than the stuff that's being shoved down your throat.

Start thinking about the power that has been given to you — the authority, the dominion and the power as a human being that is already instilled in you before you ever came out your mother's womb.

You have a purpose to fulfill, and, in that purpose, you must *Know Who You Are*, or you will never recognize that purpose. So, our thinking is crucial, it's pertinent because as a person thinks so is that person, and what is inside of the person is what comes out of the person.

The Bible says that death and life is in the power of the tongue and they that love it shall eat the fruit thereof. That means the things that you speak are the things that you're going to eat. You ever heard the saying, "You are what you eat"? That's what that is talking about. What you put in is what's going to come out. So, if you're indoctrinated, if you are brainwashed, if you have been conditioned to think this way or that way, but it's not really you, you are going to be on this never-ending wheel on this never-ending cycle that was built for you before you were born.

So, here's your options. You can either look at life right now and start creating your own definitions and creating your own life based off your own thoughts and ideas, or you can continue to run on the wheel that was built for you before you were here, and you can continue in the cycle of thinking other people's thoughts, being conditioned to do and to say and to wear and to be and behave in certain ways.

Both of these opportunities were given to you before you were born. The wheel was built before you were born, and you were given power, authority, and dominion before you were born. You have to make a choice, a decision. Do I stay on the wheel that was built for me that is a never-ending wheel that goes absolutely nowhere? Or you can make a choice to go with the power authority and dominion that was also provided for you before you were ever here. So, it is a choice and a decision that we have to make, and it all begins with *reDefining Thought*.

Joshua: I'ma stop it right there. Because that's the perfect advice that I believe you can give to these people that are struggling with thinking for themselves and knowing who they are. People that are stuck in that same condition of, the same social circle, the same worldly aspect of life. Thank you, brother.

Brian: Thank you for having me.

Joshua: Oh, aren't you going to be setting up a podcast soon?

Brian: Oh, under the direction of my brother and family members, who know I like to talk. They told me I should start a podcast before I even knew what a podcast was. Under the direction of all those different advisors, we have soon to come *Kingdom Purpose*. That in itself kind of articulates what I'm trying to express, whether it be business, whether it be personal, relationship, whether it be social. Every aspect that you can really think of that brings elevation, growth, and development.

It goes hand in hand with r*eDefining Thought*, but then, I guess once you get to a place where you start thinking for yourself, when you know that you need to r*eDefine Thought*, you *Know Who You Are*, and you know who you belong to, then you're in a position now where you need to figure out what your purpose is.

And in the process of doing that, it needs to be a *Kingdom Purpose*, not a worldly purpose. Not a pointless purpose, not a purpose that's just lost or all about self. Because one thing I've figured out, even now with what I'm doing, I'm investing, I'm pouring out into something that you're doing because, number one, because I believe in it, but also because I know I'm supposed to be here in order to help others.

That is the whole purpose of finding purpose, is to know that purpose is to assist other people and not yourself. This is not about selfishness; this is not about greed. Your purpose, that you are here to fulfill for the world, is going to be something that's here for other people. If you get to a place where you don't understand that, then you're not ready. You do not understand purpose at all if you think that your purpose is fulfilling self. Your purpose that you are here to fulfill for the world is going to be something that's here for other people. If you get to a place where you don't understand that, you are not ready and you don't understand purpose at all. If you think purpose is fulfilling self, you've missed the whole boat. You're on the side of the seashore, and it's already gone up the water.

You're lost, and you don't understand. And it took me thirty-seven years to figure out that everything that I have is for somebody else. Everything that I possess is for somebody else. The purpose that has been placed inside of me.

And again, it doesn't matter what you believe or don't believe. It doesn't matter what you believe or don't believe. Purpose is purpose. And that purpose is always going to be for somebody else. Always. It's never going to be for self. Now, self will absolutely benefit because you are doing for others. There's always going to be a benefit because that is what seed time and harvest is really about. It's not about all that silly stuff that you are hearing. That's what it is really about.

When you have seed and you scatter it, increase is coming. But when you withhold the seed, poverty is coming. That's Bible. When you have seed and you scatter it, there is increase. When you hold on to seed, it tends to poverty, and that's true.

So, when you have purpose, you need to understand that your God given purpose — again, I don't care what you believe — your purpose, your God given purpose is to fulfill purpose. And when you're fulfilling purpose, it's always going to be elevating, growing up and developing, helping and assisting someone else. And in the process of doing that, you yourself will begin to elevate and develop and grow and mature and be blessed in the process.

But everything that we have is for somebody else. So, long tangent, *Kingdom Purpose*.

Joshua: Got to be a giver.

Brian: Got to be a giver.

Joshua: Brian said it best when he said, "First, you must *Know Who You Are*."

Many continue to live their life based on the views of the world. But that's not who you are; that is who you have become by adjusting to fit the world's definition of who the world wants you to be. Don't allow the world to define you. *reDefine Thought*.

If you want to *Know Who You Are*, then lean on <u>Truth</u>. Just like Brian said, the Word is Truth.

So, what does the Word have to say about who you are?

- 1 Corinthians 3:16 says we are God's temple and that God's Spirit dwells in you.
- 2 Timothy 1:7 states that God gave us a spirit not of fear but of power and love and self-control.

Who do we belong to?

- 1 Corinthians 6:19 Do you not know that your body is a temple of the Holy Spirit within you, whom you have from God? You are not your own.
- Ephesians 1:5 states that He predestined us for adoption to himself as sons through Jesus Christ, according to the purpose of his will.
- John 1:12 But to all who did receive him, who believed in his name, he gave the right to become children of God.

We are much more than the stereotypical judgment this world places on us. We are more than the environment we grew up in. And we definitely are more than the negative things we tell ourselves.

We must speak life, not death. Speak love, not harm. This is important, because whatever seed you choose to water, that seed will bloom in your life. Choose your focus wisely.

Like Brian said, we could be our best friend or our worst enemy.

And lastly, find your *Kingdom Purpose*.

I want to thank Brian again for blessing us with his wisdom, and I want to leave the listeners with this:

1. Love God completely.
2. Love yourself correctly.
3. Love others compassionately.

And I guarantee this recipe will benefit your life in many ways. God bless.

With the power to *reDefine Thought*,

JOSHUA B. HAYES
Kingdom Ambassador

Notes:

Conclusion

I truly pray that you realize how extremely important studying is to show yourself approved and rightly dividing the Word of Truth is for you and your family.

You must begin to build a real relationship with God for yourself and to seek first the Kingdom of God and His righteousness so all the necessities of life will be added unto you.

I understand that this is a lot to take in, but I also believe that you have the authority, dominion, and power to overcome any fear or confusion that may attempt to distract you from the Truth.

The Bible declares that God is the same yesterday, today, and forever.

I was having a conversation with my brother recently, and this verse came up. He stated something so profound that I must share it with you.

I was explaining to him that the Devil is not an originator of anything, and that he just takes God's Word and plans and distorts, contradicts, and/or changes it to fit his own demonic and Satanic agenda.

Then my brother Joshua said, "The Bible says that God is the same yesterday, today, and forever, right?" Then he added, "Well then, the Devil is the same yesterday, today, and forever, too."

This is an extremely powerful understanding to have of your enemy, opposition, and adversary. Satan has no new tricks and is nothing more than a wannabe copycat of the Creator. This is how he used the contradiction of God's Word to hustle and con Adam and Eve out of their spiritual position by enticing them with a natural deception.

We covered the transition of power in the Book of Genesis in *The Garden*, how important it is that you <u>Know Who You Are</u> and provided you with a thorough explanation of your <u>*Rightful Position*</u> and the original intent.

Jesus only preached one message, and the Bible is clear about this one message:

This *Gospel of the Kingdom* must be preached to all nations as a witness.

<u>*Jesus is NOT a Religion,*</u> and <u>*Religion is NOT Relationship*</u>! <u>Religion is a destroyer of Truth!</u>

A lot of people are full of fear, confused, and <u>*Unequally Yoked and MANipulated*</u> into believing the demonic and Satanic agenda of the World's System, which only comes to steal, kill, and destroy your true identity.

You must *<u>Escape the Pig Pen</u>* mentality and mindset, get out of the mud of this World's System, and make it a point to get back to your Father's House, where you initially were before the willful disobedience of man.

This is your rebirth and how you are born again. This is the restoration and the renewing of the mind that enables you to re*<u>Define Thought</u>* and transition from the World's System back to the *Kingdom* where you belong.

Conclusion

If pastors, preachers, deacons, ministers, bishops, elders, priests, and the leaders in positions with platforms spent the same amount of time talking about what Jesus preached, instructed, and directed us to do as they spend talking only about Him, we would be a lot closer to His return.

If they spent the same amount time preaching, teaching, and healing with the Word of God and a clear biblical understanding of salvation as they spend on tithes and offerings, we would be a lot closer to Truth.

It is extremely unfortunate that, with a church or mosque on almost every major corner, we still have not accomplished true unity unless it is to deceive and manipulate God's people for selfishness and greed.

The number one reason churches are suffering today is because they lack *Acts*.

The Acts of the Apostles and Genesis Chapter 11 tell us everything we need to know about *The True Power of Unity*.

Take time to read Genesis Chapter 11 and the Book of Acts and ask yourself:

1. Where are the miracles?
2. Where is the power?
3. What happened to the importance of unity?
4. What happened to the many souls being saved?
5. Why is there lack?
6. Where is the Holy Spirit?
7. Where are the results of the multitudes?

Read Isaiah 9:6-7, Matthew 4:17, 24:14, and Luke 17:20-21 and ask yourself:

1. Why is the King and the Kingdom not being preached every time Jesus is mentioned if it is the only message He ever preached and what He instructed us to do for His return?

Read 2 Corinthians 5:17-21 and Ephesians 6:10-20 and ask yourself:

1. What is an ambassador?
2. Where are the ambassadors for the Kingdom of God today?

As representatives of the King, we must:

- Get *Back to the Garden* mentality and mindset.
- Get back to the *Way*, the *Truth*, and the *Life.*
- Get Back to the *Kingdom of God* to fulfill *Kingdom Purpose.*

I sacrifice myself and my well-being daily to provide you with the Truth because only the Truth will make you and your family free from the traditions and foolishness of men.

I pray your eyes are open to see and your ears are open to hear what thus saith the Lord.

There will no longer be any excuses for a lackluster life when you have been provided access and equipped with all the tools that are readily available.

Let God be the Truth and every man a liar! Read your Bible for yourself!

Conclusion

I invest my time writing in obedience to empower and encourage your elevation, growth, and development ultimately so that **YOU KNOW WHO YOU ARE** and the authority, dominion, and power you possess in, by, and through God the Father, Jesus the Christ, and the Holy Spirit united as one.

I pray you and your family walk in your blessings and in the Truth.

Sincerely and respectfully,

Brian P. Lucas
BRIAN P. LUCAS
Kingdom Ambassador

Kingdom Ambassador: An official representative sent by God to the World's System to promote and exemplify the *Kingdom* and the *Culture of the Kingdom* in word and action, to teach a *Kingdom Mentality and Kingdom Mindset* to fulfill purpose – *Kingdom Purpose*!

Why Jesus?

Why Did Jesus Come?   Luke 19:10 / John 10:10

For the Son of man [Jesus] is come to seek and to save that which was lost.

The thief comes not, but for to steal, and to kill, and to destroy: I [Jesus] am come that they might have life, and that they might have [life] more abundantly.

Why Do I Need Jesus?   Matthew 28:18 / John 14:6
John 10:9

And Jesus came and spake unto them, saying, All power is given unto [Jesus] in heaven and in earth.

Jesus saith unto him, I am the way, the truth, and the life: no person comes unto the Father [God], but by [Jesus].

I [Jesus] am the door: by [Jesus] if any [person] enters in, [that person] shall be saved, and shall go in and out, and find pasture.

Jesus or the World?   Mark 8:35-37

For whosoever will save their life shall lose their life; but whosoever shall lose their life for [Jesus] sake and the gospel's, the same shall save their life. For what shall it profit a [person], if they shall gain the whole world, and lose their own soul?

Salvation

For those of you who are not saved, simply read the verses below and *Make It Personal* by adding your name in the spaces provided. You will see how simple it is to receive the greatest gift that God has provided you since the fall of man.

Luke 19:10

For the Son of man [Jesus] has come to seek and to save _____ which was lost.

Romans 10:9-10

That if _____ shalt confess with _____'s mouth the Lord Jesus, and shalt believe in _____'s heart that God has raised [Jesus] from the dead, _____ shalt be saved. For with the heart _____ believes unto righteousness; and with _____'s mouth confession is made unto salvation.

John 3: 16-18

For God so loved _____, that [God] gave his only begotten Son [Jesus] that if _____ believes in [Jesus] _____ should not perish but have everlasting life. For God did not send his Son [Jesus] into the world to condemn _____; but that _____ through [Jesus] might be saved. If _____ believes on [Jesus] _____ is not condemned: but if _____ does not believe [in Jesus] then _____ is condemned already, because _____ has not believed in the name of [Jesus] the only begotten Son of God.

Please realize that all the things people have conditioned and brainwashed us to think about salvation are nowhere to be found in these verses.

We don't need religion, rules, regulations, traditions of men, priests, sprinkles of water, Hail Marys, incense, statues, animals, yoga, science, the universe, or any of the other foolishness they use to control and enslave us and keep us ignorant of Truth.

God's Word is Truth, and every man a liar. This is yet another reason why it is extremely important for you study to show yourself approved and allow the Spirit of God (not man) to rightly divide the Word of Truth for you.

For those of you who are already saved, my prayer is that you understand your daily assignment to seek and save the lost and bring them back home to their Father's House. This is how you empower yourself and others to fulfill *Kingdom Purpose*.

About the Author

Most importantly, above anything and everything else, I believe in and I trust the God in Heaven, who is the God of the Bible. I believe in God the Father, Jesus the Christ, and the Holy Spirit. I believe that Jesus is the Son of God and that Jesus died on the cross for my sins, transgressions, and unrighteousness. I believe in the resurrection, that Jesus was raised from the dead and that Jesus now sits on the right hand of God the Father with all power in Heaven and on Earth. I respectfully believe without compromise, doubts, or any second thoughts that Jesus is the one and only way to God the Father and that Jesus is the one and only way to receive Salvation and Forgiveness by the Mercy and Grace of God.

Now, am I an angel, holier than thou, full of righteousness by my own power, religious, or perfect? No!

Frankly, if I were or if anyone else actually could be, then there would be no need for Jesus or a Savior, because we would just press our holiness button and save ourselves.

I am nothing without God; this book and everything else I possess belongs to God, so I refuse to compromise on my faith and belief in God.

I am but a lonely voice in the wilderness that has experienced my own personal road to Damascus and has been awakened to a glimpse of the truth that every human being searches for.

One great thing about truth is that it is always true. Whether it's coming from a doctor or a janitor, a multi-millionaire or someone living in poverty, someone driving a luxury car or someone riding a bicycle, a dope dealer on the corner or a preacher behind the pulpit, the truth is always the truth!

Truth in word will always resonate with those who are seeking it. My birds will know my feathers and flock with me, and the sheep I am responsible for will know my voice. I will resonate with them, and they will resonate with me.

I am that I am, not what the world tells me or attempts to market and advertise me to be.

My life forever changed when I came to the simple conclusion that the world owes me nothing and that I am not entitled to anything outside of my faith that I have not worked for or willed my way.

I now understand the importance of having eyes to see and ears to hear, which enable me to see through the deception the world consistently promotes to the walking blind, who have their eyes wide shut.

I strongly believe that ethics, morals, and character still mean something today, no matter what this new world is shoving down our throats!

I promote unity over division, I support equality over slavery, and I respect hard work and not laziness.

Mentality and mindset are key: stand for something, or you will fall for anything!

About the Author

Here is my bio summed up:

I once was lost, but now I am found; I once was blind, but now I see.

My only goal and purpose in life is to open the eyes of as many people as possible while I am still here, so that each day I am hopefully putting a smile on God's face.

Every day, I want to imagine God saying, "Well done, good and faithful servant."

I am that I am because of who Jesus is.

I have what I have because of what Jesus has.

I can do what I do because of what Jesus did for me on the cross.

I am nothing without Jesus!

Every experience and accomplishment I am blessed to possess and all my joy come from the aforementioned.

Sincerely and respectfully,

Brian P. Lucas
BRIAN P. LUCAS

Author: Brian P. Lucas

Discover the quickest, easiest, most convenient way to reach your personal goals in life, by living on your own terms and by your own definitions and ultimately determining your own personal definition of perfection. If you are ready to find out who you really are and begin to live by your own definitions, and you are truly interested in succeeding and utilizing a system that's proven to work, this may be the book for you.

Author: Brian P. Lucas

Each and every day, seeds are being planted, and it is up to us to determine exactly how each seed will take root and manifest in our personal lives. The Harvest is dictated by the ground in which the seed is planted. If the ground is good, then the Harvest has the potential to be great. We must empower the Good Ground in our lives to produce a Great Harvest for our families and future generations to come.

Author: Brian P. Lucas

Multiple efforts focused on the same goals will reap multiple rewards and truly produce the results of unity. Unity begins with you, and the power of unity eliminates lack, pride, and most importantly, division. To divide is to conquer, and division only destroys and brings destruction to you and your family. Unity is the key, and nothing will be withheld from those who possess The True Power of Unity.

Author: Brian P. Lucas

Simply Believe highlights John's Walk with Jesus in an easy-to-read format with a purposely repetitive verse-by-verse breakdown.

Brian P. Lucas provides you with a direct and engaging commentary to empower you to have a greater understanding of The Gospel According to St. John.

God is Love, and God loves you.

Discover the gift of Truth that only God will provide, and Simply Believe.

Author: Brian P. Lucas

God has a specific message for every one of us, if we simply have the ears to hear His voice when He speaks.

Do not be fooled by the World's System and the religious puppets who attempt to dictate and deteriorate the message that God has for you.

People are searching for the Truth because it is only the Truth that brings real freedom.

We must understand God's Message to Teach, Preach, and Heal.

Author: Brian P. Lucas

Honesty opens our eyes to see *Truth*, and the *Truth* brings us revelation and confirmation that forces us to get out of our own comfort zones.

Elevation, growth, and development are key to building successful relationships, and we must be knowledgeable of one another's motives in the process.

We must make it a point to eliminate the toxic relationships in our lives and find our purpose.

Author: Brian P. Lucas

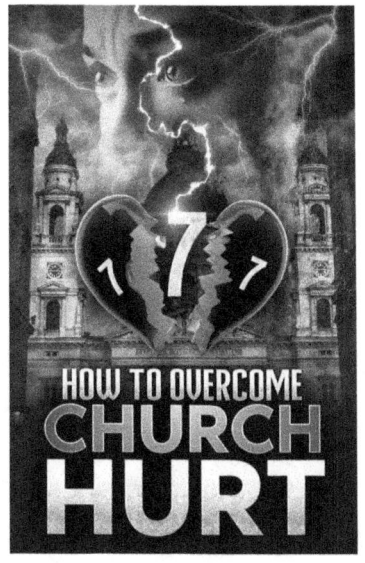

Church Hurt is real, and it empowers division to destroy unity.

Many people have turned away from God because of the hurt, pain, abuse, and rejection of Man. Whether it be *condemnation, discrimination,* and *disrespect,* or whispers, stares, pointed fingers, mockery, and *gossip,* we must not allow ourselves to be distracted.

You cannot allow the ignorance and failures of others to dictate your personal relationship with God. Man is *not* God and God is *not* Man. Man will fail you, but God will *never* fail you, leave you, or forsake you.

The lack of *biblical leadership* in the church has destroyed many people's walk with God because they mistakenly base their value of God on the actions of Man. We spend too much time and energy focused on Man, and the rules, regulations, and traditions of men, which are nothing more than purposeful distractions to keep us from experiencing God's best.

Church Hurt is a tool that Satan uses to keep you from trusting God.

Knowing *How to Overcome Church Hurt* is extremely important for your elevation, growth, and development.

www.ingramcontent.com/pod-product-compliance
Lightning Source LLC
Chambersburg PA
CBHW050611100526
44585CB00034B/1259